SA GREATS

ALLAN NEED & ROGER HENDERSON

A catalogue record for this book is available from the National Library of Australia

SA Greats: They changed South Australia, and the world
Need, Allan and Henderson, Roger (Authors)
ISBN 978-1-922337-54-2

Cover and book design by Green Hill Publishing

Typeset Whitman 11/15

Disclaimer

The material in this publication is of the nature of general comment only and does not represent professional advice. It is not intended to provide specific guidance for particular circumstances, and it should not be relied on as the basis for any decision to take action or not take action on any matter, which it covers.

Attributions

Photo J M Coetzee courtesy of Mariusz Kubik, http://www.mariuszkubik.pl
Photo Max Schubert tasting wine courtesy of
Treasury Wine Estates, https://www.tweglobal.com/
Tom Angove courtesy of Victoria Angove, Victoria.Angove@angove.com.au

FOREWORD

There have always been many reasons to come to South Australia. The first inhabitants were no doubt attracted by plentiful food along the coasts and rivers, a warm climate and a habitat which was pleasantly wooded. In more recent times, people came to South Australia from Britain in response to advertising for settlers. They were attracted by different things – initially land for farming, mineral wealth, a welcoming political system, and of course the mild Mediterranean climate. Even more recently, the welcome has been extended, and people from all round the world have come to call South Australia home. Some of them could have chosen anywhere in the world to live, but they come here to further enrich themselves in what is now a diverse and progressive culture.

Inspired by the seventeenth century Age of Reason and the eighteenth century Age of Enlightenment, many people with vision have contributed their ideas to South Australia. Matthew Flinders is a good example. His mapping defined the continent of Australia; it was based on science and technology, following people like Newton, Laplace, Liebniz, Halley and others. During his exploration, Flinders experimented with the magnetic compass, and the Royal Navy used his data in developing the 'Flinders Bar' to correct for deviations due to iron in sailing ships. He was also concerned with social justice. In 1803, he named Cape Wilberforce in Queensland after William Wilberforce, the politician who did so much to abolish slavery in the British Empire. They maintained contact, and in 1811 Flinders received an offer of help from William in his negotiations with the Navy over his pension.

Immigrants of the twenty-first century continue to add to these ideals, and South Australia has wisely welcomed anyone who has a vision of a better life. In 2019, South Australia installed the world's biggest battery in an attempt to lead the way to reducing carbon dioxide production and slow global warming.

It is not too ambitious to hope that South Australians will make further technical and social progress, and that the impact of such things as racism, disability afflictions, gender dysphoria, domestic violence, third-generation unemployment and suffering during terminal illness will be ameliorated. Perhaps it is time to be kinder to ourselves now that the plebiscite on same-sex marriage has shown how Australians can respect each other's differences, and parliaments are learning to deal more leniently with such issues as euthanasia and the private lives of sex workers.

This book presents a number of the South Australians who have been world leaders in social development. The information comes from various sources: from books (listed at the end), contemporaneous press articles, personal communications and the anonymous contributors to Wikipedia. Any errors are ours.

Only some of the people who have contributed to our current good fortune are listed here, and the list is a subjective one. An omission is by no means meant to belittle anyone who has come here, worked, reproduced, and passed on their own vision of what the good life should be.

CONTENTS

MATTHEW FLINDERS 1774–1814

CARTOGRAPHER OF THE SOUTHERN COAST OF AUSTRALIA

Captain Matthew Flinders was an English navigator and mapmaker who led the first circumnavigation of Australia and identified it as an 'island continent'. He was the first to map much of the coastline of South Australia.

Flinders made three voyages to the Southern Ocean between 1791 and 1803. In the second voyage George Bass and Flinders confirmed that Van Diemen's Land (now Tasmania) was an island, and the strait between it and the mainland provided a quicker passage from Europe to Port Jackson (now Sydney). In the third voyage, Flinders circumnavigated the mainland of what he was to call Australia, accompanied by Aboriginal man Bungaree.

Heading back to England in 1803, Flinders' vessel needed urgent repairs at Isle de France (Mauritius). Although Britain and France were at war, Flinders thought the scientific nature of his work would ensure safe passage, but the suspicious Governor kept him under arrest for more than six years. While he was in captivity, he recorded details of his voyages for future publication, and put forward his rationale for naming the new continent 'Australia', as an umbrella term for New Holland and New South Wales – a suggestion taken up later by Governor Macquarie.

However, Flinders' health had suffered and although he reached home in 1810, he did not live to see the success of his widely praised book and atlas, *A Voyage to Terra Australis*. By the mid-19th century the location of his grave was lost, but in January 2019 archaeologists excavating a former burial ground near London's Euston railway station, for the HS2 project, reported that his remains had been identified.

Matthew Flinders was born in Donington, Lincolnshire, England, the son of Matthew Flinders, a surgeon, and his wife Susannah, née Ward. He was educated at Cowley's Charity School, Donington, from 1780 and then at the Reverend John Shinglar's Grammar School at Horbling in Lincolnshire.

In his own words, he was 'induced to go to sea against the wishes of my friends from reading *Robinson Crusoe*', and in 1790, at the age of fifteen, he joined the Royal Navy. Initially serving on HMS *Alert*, he transferred to HMS *Scipio*, and in July 1790 was made midshipman on HMS *Bellerophon* under Captain Pasley. In 1791, on Pasley's recommendation, he joined Captain Bligh's expedition on HMS *Providence*, transporting breadfruit from Tahiti to Jamaica. This was Bligh's second 'breadfruit voyage' following the ill-fated voyage of the *Bounty*.

In 1795 Flinders made his first voyage to New South Wales, and first trip to Port Jackson. He was a midshipman aboard HMS *Reliance*, which carried the newly appointed Governor of New South Wales, Captain John Hunter. On this voyage he quickly established himself as a fine navigator and cartographer, and became friends with the ship's surgeon George Bass, who was three years his senior and had been born 11 miles (18 km) from Donington.

Not long after their arrival in Port Jackson, Bass and Flinders made two expeditions in two small open boats, named *Tom Thumb* and *Tom*

Thumb II respectively. The first was to Botany Bay and Georges River; and the second, in the larger *Tom Thumb II*, south from Port Jackson to Lake Illawarra, during which expedition they had to seek shelter at Wattamolla.

In 1798, Matthew Flinders, now a lieutenant, was given command of the sloop *Norfolk* with orders 'to sail beyond Furneaux's Islands, and, should a strait be found, pass through it, and return by the south end of Van Diemen's Land'. His discovery of the passage between the Australian mainland and Tasmania enabled savings of several days on the journey from England. It was named Bass Strait, after his close friend. In honour of this discovery, the largest island in Bass Strait was later named Flinders Island. The town of Flinders near the mouth of Western Port also commemorates the discovery by Bass and Flinders of that bay and port, on 4 January 1798. Flinders never entered Western Port, and passed Cape Schanck only on 3 May 1802.

On 17 July 1799, Flinders once more set sail on *Norfolk*. This time he headed north, and arrived in Moreton Bay between modern-day Redcliffe and Brighton. He touched down at Pumicestone Passage, Redcliffe and Coochiemudlo Island, and also rowed ashore at Clontarf. During this visit he named Redcliffe after the Red Cliffs. In March 1800, Flinders rejoined *Reliance* and set sail for England.

Flinders' work had come to the attention of many of the scientists of the day, in particular the influential Sir Joseph Banks, to whom Flinders dedicated his *Observations on the Coasts of Van Diemen's Land, on Bass's Strait, etc.* Banks used his influence with Earl Spencer to convince the Admiralty of the importance of an expedition to chart the coastline of New Holland. As a result, in January 1801 Flinders was given command of HMS *Investigator*, a 334-ton sloop, and promoted to Commander the following month.

On 17 April 1801, Flinders married his long-time friend Ann Chappelle (1772–1852). He had hoped to bring her with him to Port Jackson, but the Admiralty had strict rules against wives accompanying captains. Flinders brought Ann on board ship and planned to ignore the rules, but the Admiralty learned of his plans and he was severely chastised for his bad judgement and told he must remove her from the ship. It did not help that the ship had run aground while Ann was aboard. The Admiralty's displeasure is well documented in correspondence between Flinders and his chief benefactor, Sir Joseph Banks, in May 1801:

> *I have but time to tell you that the news of your marriage, which was published in the Lincoln paper, has reached me. The Lords of the Admiralty have heard also that Mrs. Flinders is on board the Investigator, and that you have some thought of carrying her to sea with you. This I was very sorry to hear, and if that is the case I beg to give you my advice by no means to adventure to measures so contrary to the regulations and the discipline of the Navy; for I am convinced by language I have heard, that their Lordships will, if they hear of her being in New South Wales, immediately order you to be superseded, whatever may be the consequences, and in all likelihood order Mr. Grant to finish the survey.*

Ann was obliged to stay in England and did not see her husband for nine years because of his imprisonment on the Isle de France. When they finally reunited, Matthew and Ann had one daughter, Anne (1812–1892), who later married William Petrie (1821–1908). In 1853, the governments of New South Wales and Victoria bequeathed a belated pension to her (deceased) mother of £100 per year, to go to surviving issue of the union. This she accepted on behalf of her young son, William Matthew Flinders Petrie, who would go on to become an accomplished archaeologist and Egyptologist.

Aboard *Investigator*, Flinders reached and named Cape Leeuwin on 6 December 1801, and proceeded to make a survey along the southern coast of the Australian mainland. On his way he stopped in at Oyster Harbour, Western Australia. There he found a copper plate that Captain Christopher Dixson, on *Elligood*, had left the year before. It was inscribed: 'Aug. 27 1800. Chr Dixson, ship Elligood'.

On 8 April 1802, while sailing east, Flinders sighted *Géographe*, a French corvette commanded by the explorer Nicolas Baudin, who was on a similar expedition for his Government. Both men of science, Flinders and Baudin met and exchanged details of their discoveries. Flinders named the nearby bay Encounter Bay.

Proceeding along the coast, Flinders explored Port Phillip which, unbeknownst to him, had been discovered only ten weeks earlier by John Murray aboard HMS *Lady Nelson*. Flinders scaled Arthur's Seat, the highest point near the shores of the southernmost parts of the bay, where the ship had entered through The Heads. From there he saw a vast view of the surrounding land and bays. He reported back to Governor King that the land had 'a pleasing and, in many parts, a fertile appearance'. After scaling the You Yangs to the northwest on 1 May, he stated: 'I left the ship's name on a scroll of paper, deposited in a small pile of stones upon the top of the peak'. He was drawing upon a British tradition of constructing a stone cairn to mark a historical location. The Matthew Flinders Cairn, which was later enlarged, is located on the upper slopes of Arthur's Seat, a short distance below Chapman's Point.

With stores running low, Flinders proceeded to Sydney and arrived on 9 May 1802. Here he was rejoined by Bungaree, the Aboriginal man who had accompanied him on his earlier coastal survey in 1799.

Having hastily prepared the ship, Flinders set sail again on 22 July, heading north and surveying the coast of Queensland. From there he passed through the Torres Strait, and explored the Gulf of Carpentaria. During this time, the ship was discovered to be badly leaking, but despite careening, they were unable to effect the necessary repairs. Reluctantly, Flinders returned to Sydney, this time via the western coast, thereby completing the circumnavigation of the continent. On the way, he jettisoned two wrought-iron anchors which were found by divers in 1973 at Middle Island, Recherche Archipelago, Western Australia. The best – a bower anchor – is on display at the South Australian Maritime Museum; the second was a stream anchor and it can be seen in Canberra at the National Museum of Australia.

The *Investigator* arrived in Sydney on 9 June 1803 and was subsequently judged to be unseaworthy, and condemned.

While not formally trained in natural philosophy (now termed physics), Flinders coined the term 'dodge tide' in reference to his 1802/3 observations that the tides in the very shallow Spencer and St Vincent's Gulfs seemed to be completely inert for several days, at select locations. Such phenomena have now also been found in the Gulf of Mexico and in the Irish Sea. In the Irish Sea and the two South Australian gulfs, a north-bound wave from the open ocean interferes non-linearly with a reflected and weaker southbound wave. This results in aperiodic and very dissipative tidal motions.

In his 1803 observations of the large tides at Broad Sound in Queensland (up to 11m range), Flinders correctly attributed this behaviour to two waves travelling north and south respectively, and meeting at Broad Sound. He postulated that the dense reef wall further offshore caused the deep ocean tide to bifurcate at the northern and southern ends of the reef, travel into shallow shelf waters, and meet at Broad Sound. These phenomena were confirmed by GI Taylor in his landmark 1919 Irish Sea analysis.

Unable to find another vessel suitable to continue his exploration, Flinders set sail for England as a passenger aboard HMS *Porpoise*. However, the ship was wrecked on Wreck Reefs, part of the Great Barrier Reef, approximately 700 miles (1,100 km) north of Sydney. Flinders navigated the ship's cutter across open sea back to Sydney, and arranged for the rescue of the remaining marooned crew. He then took command of the 29-ton schooner HMS *Cumberland* in order to return to England, but on 17 December 1803 the poor condition of the vessel forced him to put in at French-controlled Isle de France (now known as Mauritius) for repairs, just three months after Baudin had died there.

War with France had broken out again the previous May, but Flinders hoped his French passport (despite its being issued for *Investigator* and not *Cumberland*) and the scientific nature of his mission would allow him to continue on his way. However, the French

Governor, Charles Mathieu Isidore Decaen, knew about Baudin's earlier encounter with Flinders, and detained him. The relationship between the two men soured as Flinders was affronted at his treatment, and Decaen was insulted by Flinders' refusal of an invitation to dine with him and his wife.

Decaen was suspicious of the alleged scientific mission, as the *Cumberland* carried no scientists; a search of Flinders' vessel uncovered a trunk full of papers (including despatches from the New South Wales Governor, Philip Gidley King) that were not permitted under his scientific passport. Furthermore, one of King's despatches was specifically addressed to the British Admiralty, requesting more troops in case Decaen were to attack Port Jackson. Also among the papers seized were the three logs of HMS *Investigator*, of which only Volumes One and Two were returned to Flinders; they are now both held by the State Library of New South Wales. The third volume was later deposited in the Admiralty Library and is now held in the British Public Record Office.

Decaen referred the matter of Flinders' detention to the French Government; the matter was delayed not only by the long voyage, but also by the general confusion of war. Eventually, on 11 March 1806, Napoleon gave his approval, but Decaen still refused to allow Flinders' release, saying he was waiting until 'the appropriate time'. By this stage, Decaen believed Flinders' knowledge of the island's defences would have encouraged Britain to attempt to capture it. Nevertheless, in June 1809 the Royal Navy began a blockade of the island, and in June 1810 Flinders was paroled. As he travelled via the Cape of Good Hope on *Olympia*, which was taking despatches back to Britain, he received a promotion to Post Captain.

Flinders had been confined for the first few months of his captivity, but he was later afforded greater freedom to move around the island and access his papers. In November 1804 he sent back to England the first map of the land mass he had charted (Y46/1). This was the only map made by Flinders where he used the name AUSTRALIA (all capitals) for the title, and the first known time he used the word Australia.

Due to the delay caused by his lengthy confinement, the first published map of the Australian continent was the Freycinet Map of 1811, a product of the Baudin expedition.

Flinders finally returned to England in October 1810. He was in poor health, but immediately resumed work on preparing *A Voyage to Terra Australis* and his atlas of maps for publication. This book was first published in London in July 1814, and as was common at the time, the full title was given as a synoptic description:

A Voyage to Terra Australis: undertaken for the purpose of completing the discovery of that vast country, and prosecuted in the years 1801, 1802, and 1803 in His Majesty's ship the Investigator, and subsequently in the armed vessel Porpoise and Cumberland Schooner. With an account of the shipwreck of the Porpoise, arrival of the Cumberland at Mauritius, and imprisonment of the commander during six years and a half in that island.

Original copies of the *Atlas to Flinders' Voyage to Terra Australis* are held at the Mitchell Library in Sydney as a portfolio that accompanied the book, and included engravings of 16 maps, four plates of views and ten plates of Australian flora. The book was republished in three volumes in 1964, accompanied by a reproduction of the portfolio. Flinders' map of *Terra Australis* was first published in January 1814 and the remaining maps were published before his atlas and book.

Flinders died at the age of 40, on 19 July 1814, probably from kidney failure. It was the day after the book and atlas was published. On 23 July, he was interred in the burial ground of St James's Church, Piccadilly, which was located some way from the church, beside Hampstead Road, Camden, London. The burial ground was in use from 1790 until 1853. By 1852, the location of the grave had been forgotten due to alterations to the burial ground.

In 1878, the cemetery became St James's Gardens, Camden, and by then only a few gravestones lined the edges of the park. The gardens were located between Hampstead Road and Euston railway station, and a part of them was built over when Euston Station was expanded. It is thought that Flinders' grave lay under a platform at the station. The Gardens were closed to the public in 2017. The grave was re-located in January 2019 by archaeologists working on the High Speed 2 rail project, which required the expansion of Euston Station. Flinders' coffin was identified by its well-preserved lead coffin plate. After examination by osteo-archaeologists, it is proposed that his remains be re-buried at a site to be decided.

Flinders' map Y46/1 was never 'lost'. It had been stored and recorded by the UK Hydrographic Office before 1828. Geoffrey C. Ingleton mentioned Y46/1 on page 438 of his book *Matthew Flinders Navigator and Chartmaker*. By 1987 every library in Australia had access to a microfiche copy of Flinders Y46/1. In 2001–2002 the Mitchell Library in Sydney displayed Y46/1 at their exhibition entitled *Matthew Flinders – The Ultimate Voyage*. Paul Brunton called Y46/1 'the memorial of the great naval explorer Matthew Flinders'.

The first hard copy of Y46/1 and its cartouche was retrieved from the UK Hydrographic Office (Taunton, Somerset) by historian Bill Fairbanks in 2004. In London on 2 April 2004, copies of the chart were presented by three of Matthew Flinders' descendants to the Governor of New South Wales, to be presented in turn to the people of Australia through their Parliaments by 14 November, the 200th anniversary of the chart leaving Mauritius. This celebration marked the first formal recognition of the naming of Australia.

Flinders was not the first to use the word 'Australia', nor was he the first to apply the name specifically to the continent. He owned a copy of Alexander Dalrymple's 1771 book *An Historical Collection of Voyages and Discoveries in the South Pacific Ocean*, and it seems likely he borrowed it from there; but he applied it specifically to the continent, not the whole South Pacific region. In 1804 he wrote to his brother: 'I call the whole island Australia, or Terra Australis.' Later that year he wrote to Sir Joseph Banks and mentioned 'my general chart of Australia' - a map Flinders had constructed from all the information he had accumulated while he was in Australian waters and finished while he was detained by the French in Mauritius. In his letter to Banks, Flinders explained:

The propriety of the name Australia or Terra Australis, which I have applied to the whole body of what has generally been called New Holland, must be submitted to the approbation of the Admiralty and the learned in geography. It seems to me an inconsistent thing that captain Cook's New South Wales should be absorbed in the New Holland of the Dutch, and therefore I have reverted to the original name Terra Australis or the Great South Land, by which it was distinguished even by the Dutch during the 17th century; for it appears that it was not until some time after Tasman's second voyage that the name New Holland was first applied, and then it was long before it displaced T'Zuydt Landt in the charts, and could not extend to what was not yet known to have existence; New South Wales, therefore, ought to remain distinct from New Holland; but as it is requisite that the whole body should have one general name, since it is now known (if there is no great error in the Dutch part) that it is certainly all one land, so I judge, that one less exception-able to all parties and on all accounts cannot be found than that now applied.

Flinders continued to promote the use of the word until his arrival in London in 1810. Here he found that Banks did not approve of the name and had not unpacked the chart he had sent him, and that 'New Holland' and 'Terra Australis' were still in general use. As a result, a book by Flinders was published under the title *A Voyage to Terra Australis*, despite his objections. The final proofs were brought to him on his deathbed, but he was unconscious. The book was published on 18 July 1814, but Flinders did not regain consciousness and died the next day, never knowing that his name for the continent would be accepted.

In a draft introduction to Flinders' *Voyage*, Banks referred to the map published by Melchisédech Thévenot in *Relations des Divers*

Voyages (1663). It was made well-known to English readers by Emanuel Bowen's adaptation of it - *A Complete Map of the Southern Continent* – which was published in John Campbell's editions of John Harris's *Navigantium atque Itinerantium Bibliotheca, or Voyages and Travels* (1744–48, and 1764).

Flinders' book was widely read and this gave the term 'Australia' general currency. Lachlan Macquarie, Governor of New South Wales, became aware of Flinders' preference for the name Australia and used it in his dispatches to England. On 12 December 1817 he recommended to the Colonial Office that it be officially adopted. In 1824, the British Admiralty agreed that the continent should be known officially as Australia.

Although he never used his own name for any feature in all his discoveries, Flinders' name is now associated with over 100 geographical features and places in Australia, including Flinders Island in Bass Strait, but not Flinders Island in South Australia, which he named for his younger brother, Samuel Flinders.

Flinders is seen as being particularly important in South Australia, where he is considered the main explorer of the state. Landmarks named after him in South Australia include the Flinders Ranges and Flinders Ranges National Park, Flinders Column at Mount Lofty, Flinders Chase National Park on Kangaroo Island, Flinders University, Flinders Medical Centre, the suburb Flinders Park and Flinders Street in Adelaide. In Victoria, eponymous places include Flinders Peak, Flinders Street in Melbourne, the suburb of Flinders, the federal electorate of Flinders, and the Matthew Flinders Girls Secondary College in Geelong. Flinders Bay in Western Australia and Flinders Way in Canberra also commemorate Matthew Flinders. Educational institutions named after him include Flinders Park Primary School in South Australia, and Matthew Flinders Anglican College on the Sunshine Coast in Queensland. A former electoral district of the Queensland Parliament was named Flinders. There are also Flinders Highways in both Queensland and South Australia.

Bass and Flinders Point in the southernmost part of Cronulla in New South Wales features a monument to George Bass and Matthew Flinders, who explored the Port Hacking estuary.

Australia holds a large collection of statues erected in Flinders' honour. In his native England, the first statue of Flinders was erected on 16 March 2006 (his birthday) in his hometown of Donington. The statue also depicts his beloved cat Trim, who accompanied him on his voyages. In July 2014, on the 200th anniversary of his death, a large bronze statue of Flinders by the sculptor Mark Richards was unveiled at Australia House, London, by Prince William, Duke of Cambridge; it was later installed at Euston Station near the presumed location of his grave.

Flinders' proposal for the use of iron bars to compensate for the magnetic deviations caused by iron on board a ship resulted in their being known as 'Flinders bars'.

Flinders was Sir John Franklin's cousin by marriage (John's mother Hannah was the sister of Matthew's stepmother Elizabeth); he instilled in Franklin a love for navigating, and took his cousin with him on his voyage aboard *Investigator*.

In 1964 he was honoured on a postage stamp issued by the Postmaster-General's Department; again in 1980; and in 1998 with George Bass.

Flindersia is a genus of 14 species of tree in the citrus family. It was named by *Investigator*'s botanist, Robert Brown, in honour of Matthew Flinders.

Flinders landed on Coochiemudlo Island on 19 July 1799, while he was searching for a river in the southern part of Moreton Bay, Queensland, Australia. The island's residents celebrate Flinders Day annually, to commemorate the landing. The celebrations are usually held on a weekend near 19 July, the actual date of the landing.

MATTHEW FLINDERS' PUBLICATIONS INCLUDE:

A Voyage to Terra Australis, with an accompanying Atlas. 2 vol. - London: G & W Nicol, 18 July 1814

Australia Circumnavigated: The Journal of HMS Investigator, 1801-1803. Edited by Kenneth Morgan, 2 vols, The Hakluyt Society, London, 2015.[2]

Trim: Being the True Story of a Brave Seafaring Cat.

Private Journal 1803-1814. Edited with an introduction by Anthony J. Brown and Gillian Dooley. Friends of the State Library of South Australia, 2005.

Flinders, Matthew (1806). 'Observations upon the Marine Barometer, Made during the Examination of the Coasts of New Holland and New South Wales, in the Years 1801, 1802, and 1803'. *Philosophical Transactions of the Royal Society.* 96: 239-266. doi:10.1098/ rstl.1806.0012.

Flinders, Matthew (1805). 'Concerning the Differences in the Magnetic Needle, on Board the Investigator, Arising from an Alteration in the Direction of the Ship's Head'. *Philosophical Transactions of the Royal Society*

WILLIAM LIGHT 1786-1839

FOUNDER OF ADELAIDE, THE GARDEN CITY

Colonel Light was a British-Malaysian naval and army officer and a painter. He was the first Surveyor-General of the Colony of South Australia, and is famous for choosing the site of the province's capital, Adelaide, and for designing the layout of the city centre and the parklands of the 'Garden City'. The parklands were for walking and other leisure pursuits. Populous towns in England did not have these facilities at the time and Light intended to provide a model for reform.

Light was born in Kuala Kedah (now in Malaysia). He lived in Penang until the age of six, when he was sent to England to be educated. He was of Eurasian background, the son of Captain Francis Light, the Superintendent of Penang who had married Martinha Rozells, William's mother, according to the native custom. Rozells was of Portuguese or French, and Siamese or Malay descent.

At the age of 13, Light volunteered for the Royal Navy, in which he served for two years. He then travelled through Europe and India before joining the 4th Dragoons regiment of the British Army in 1808. After courageous service in Spain against Napoleon's forces during the Peninsular War, from 1809 to 1814, he served under the Duke of Wellington and went on to serve in various parts of Britain as a Captain.

In 1821, Light married E Perois in Derry, Ireland; he later lost her in tragic circumstances. In 1823 he returned to Spain to fight the French invasion as aide-de-camp to Sir Robert Wilson. He volunteered as a private in the Vigo militia, and was eventually promoted to Lieutenant-Colonel. He was badly wounded at Corunna and saved from execution by the French. After returning to England he married his second wife, Mary Bennet, natural daughter of the Duke of Richmond; the couple travelled in Europe, the Mediterranean, and Egypt.

Between 1830 and 1835 Light helped Mohammad Ali, founder of modern Egypt, to establish a Navy. He captained the Pasha's steamship *Nile* from the River Thames to Alexandria, and then served in the Egyptian Navy.

Light was initially considered for the position of Resident Commissioner of South Australia. However, this post was given to James Hurtle Fisher, and in 1836 Light was appointed Surveyor-General of the new Province. He sailed for South Australia with Maria Gandy and her brothers (his second wife having left him for another man), and some of his survey staff on the Survey Brig *Rapid*.

Light was the first to accurately chart the Port Adelaide River, and he selected the location for the City of Adelaide and designed and laid out the plan. The city centre was designed by Light to span the River Torrens, with six city squares and a figure-of-eight of open space, the Adelaide Park Lands. One of his reasons for choosing the location was the provision of rainfall by clouds drifting over the nearby Adelaide Hills, a promising indicator of the conditions required for avoidance of drought. Another was that the site was adjacent to the perennial creek grandly named the River Torrens: the supply of fresh surface water was a key requirement, and its absence had resulted in the rejection or relocation of settlement sites on Kangaroo Island, Port Lincoln and Holdfast Bay (now known as Glenelg).

When Light was designing Adelaide, his plans included 2,300 acres of parklands to surround the city. This would provide the urban population in the City of Adelaide with public walks, which were to be preserved in perpetuity.

It is sometimes claimed that Light also designed the city of Christchurch in New Zealand, but this is not possible because Light died in Adelaide in 1839, and Christchurch was not settled until 1850. However, the settlement and planning of Christchurch was based on Edward Gibbon Wakefield's theory of systematic colonisation, the principles that had been first tested with the founding of South Australia.

Light's role in founding and designing the South Australian capital is remembered as 'Light's Vision', and is commemorated with a statue (also named Light's Vision). The statue was relocated from Victoria Square to Montefiore Hill, where it now points towards the River Torrens and the southern part of the City of Adelaide.

Extracts from Light's diary in 1839 are quoted on a plaque attached to the statue, and they highlight the difficulties he faced in having this site chosen:

The reasons that led me to fix Adelaide where it is I do not expect to be generally understood or calmly judged of at present. My enemies however, by disputing their validity in every particular, have done me the good service of fixing the whole of the responsibility upon me. I am perfectly willing to bear it, and I leave it to posterity and not to them, to decide whether I am entitled to praise or to blame.

Light's survey of the City of Adelaide commenced from the corner of North Terrace and West Terrace, and there is a plaque in the vicinity of Light's and Fisher's huts and the first Land and Survey Offices. This plaque is now situated outside the main entrance of the new Royal Adelaide Hospital.

Because of Light's design, Adelaide is noted as one of the great planned metropolises. The city's grid layout, with alternating wide and narrow streets interspaced with six public squares, has made it an ideal modern city, well able to cope with traffic; and the Adelaide Park Lands that surround it provide a 'city in a park' feel to this day.

In December 1837, Light led an exploration from Adelaide, discovering and naming the (now world famous) Barossa Valley. The name is said to be a misnomer, as he meant to commemorate a site (Bar Rosa) where he fought with the British in the Peninsular War while trying to capture Cadiz; however, the more felicitous sound of 'Barossa' may have been Light's invention.

In 1838, after refusing to use less accurate surveying methods for country surveys, Light resigned from his position and formed a private company, Light, Finniss and Co, with BT Finniss, Henry Nixon, William Jacob and Robert G Thomas (these last two were among his assistants who came out on the *Rapid*). The company offered a range of services to prospective purchasers of city and country properties, and to local government bodies. In January 1839 the Land and Survey Office, and Light's adjoining hut (along with that of James Hurtle Fisher), burned down, taking some of the province's early records and many of Light's possessions with it.

Light spoke several languages and was also an artist. Many of his watercolours were published in London in 1823 and 1828, and a number of his works, including an incomplete self-portrait, are in the collection of the Art Gallery of South Australia on North Terrace.

William Light died of tuberculosis on 6 October 1839 in Adelaide, aged 53. He was buried in Light Square, one of the six squares of the City of Adelaide. A memorial to him was erected in 1843. It eroded and crumbled and was replaced in 1905 with a monumental obelisk, topped with a surveyor's theodolite, that signals his resting place. On the monument it is noted that Light is the only person legally buried after settlement within the city square.

CHARLES NAPIER STURT 1795–1869

STURT OF THE MURRAY

Captain Sturt undertook one of the greatest open boat voyages of all time, ranking with Bligh's open boat voyage of 6,500 km from the South Pacific Ocean to Timor after the mutiny on the *Bounty*. The result was to open up the south-east of Australia, and in particular the area around where Adelaide was to be established.

He led several expeditions into the interior of the continent, starting from Sydney and later from Adelaide. His expeditions traced several of the westward-flowing rivers, establishing that they all merged into the Murray River. He was trying to prove his own passionately held belief that there was an 'inland sea' at the centre of the continent.

Charles Sturt was born in Bengal, British India, the eldest son (of thirteen children) of Thomas Lenox Napier Sturt, a judge under the British East India Company. At the age of five, he was sent to live with relatives in England to be educated, and after attending a preparatory school he was sent to Harrow in 1810.

In 1812 Charles went to read with a Mr Preston near Cambridge, but his father was not wealthy and had difficulty finding the money to send him to Cambridge University, or to establish him in a profession. An aunt made an appeal to the Prince Regent and, on 9 September 1813 Sturt was gazetted as an ensign with the 39th (Dorsetshire) Regiment of Foot in the British Army.

Sturt saw action with the Duke of Wellington in the Peninsular War and against the Americans in Canada during the War of 1812; he returned to Europe a few days after the Battle of Waterloo. On 7 April 1823 he was gazetted Lieutenant, and promoted to Captain on 15 December 1825. With a detachment from his regiment, Sturt escorted convicts aboard the *Mariner* to New South Wales, arriving in Sydney on 23 May 1827.

Sturt found the conditions and climate in New South Wales much better than he expected, and he developed a great interest in the country. The Governor of New South Wales, Sir Ralph Darling, formed a high opinion of Sturt and appointed him Major of Brigade and Military Secretary. Sturt became friendly with John Oxley, Allan Cunningham, Hamilton Hume and other explorers. He was keen to explore the Australian interior, especially its rivers.

On 4 November 1828 Sturt received approval from Governor Darling to explore the area of western New South Wales. However, it was not until 10 November that the party started out. It consisted of Sturt, his servant Joseph Harris, three soldiers and eight convicts; on 27 November Sturt was joined by Hamilton Hume as his first assistant. Hume's experience proved to be very useful. A week was spent at Wellington Valley breaking in oxen and horses, and on 7 December the party made the real start into comparatively little-known country.

1828–1829 was a period of drought and there was difficulty in getting sufficient water. The courses of the Macquarie, Bogan and Castlereagh Rivers had been followed, and the Darling River had been visited, although its importance was not realised. When they came upon this river, men and animals had been without water for thirty or thirty-six hours, and the sight of it was truly wonderful. There were pelicans and wild fowl, and paths down to the water. But the water was too salty for either men or animals to drink. Sturt's obsession with finding an inland sea was, of course, re-invigorated. Luckily, Hume found a freshwater stream nearby and there was ample refreshment the following morning.

The party returned to Wellington Valley on 21 April 1829. On 21 November 1829 Governor Darling wrote to George Murray, the UK Secretary of State, that:

should it (the Murrumbidgee) unite with the Darling, and proceed to any part of the Southern Coast, within a reasonable distance, it might in the event of the land being of good quality, prove an inducement to the settlement of that part of the Country.

This turned out to be the case.

The expedition proved that northern New South Wales was not an inland sea, but deepened the mystery of where the western-flowing rivers of New South Wales went. In 1829 Governor Darling approved an expedition to solve this mystery. Sturt proposed to travel down the Murrumbidgee River, whose upper reaches had been seen by the Hume and Hovell expedition. Hume was unable to join the party, and George Macleay went in his place 'as a companion rather than as an assistant'. They carried a whaleboat that had been built in sections; in due course it was assembled, and on 7 January 1830 the eventful voyage down the Murrumbidgee began. Later in January Sturt's party reached the confluence of the Murrumbidgee and a much larger river, which Sturt named the Murray River. It was in fact the same river that Hume and Hovell had crossed further upstream and named the Hume. Several times the party was in danger from Aborigines, but Sturt always succeeded in propitiating them. Sturt then proceeded down the Murray, until he reached the river's confluence with the Darling. He had now proved that all the western-flowing rivers eventually flowed into the Murray.

In February 1830 the party reached a large lake which Sturt called Lake Alexandrina. A few days later, they reached the sea. There they made the disappointing discovery that the mouth of the Murray was a maze of lagoons and sandbars, impassable to shipping. The party then faced the ordeal of rowing back up the Murray and Murrumbidgee, against the current, in the heat of an Australian summer. Their supplies ran out, and when they reached the site of Narrandera in April, they were unable to go any further. Sturt sent two men overland in search of supplies and they returned in time to save the party from starvation; but Sturt went blind for some months and never fully recovered his health. By the time they arrived back in Sydney they had rowed and sailed nearly 2,900 kilometres of the river system.

Sturt briefly served as Commander on Norfolk Island, where mutiny was brewing among the convicts. However, in 1832 he was obliged to go to England on sick leave, and he arrived there almost completely blind. In 1833 he published his *Two Expeditions into the Interior of Southern Australia during the years 1828, 1829, 1830 and 1831*, and a second edition appeared in 1834. For the first time the public in England realised the importance of Sturt's work.

Governor Darling's somewhat tardy but appreciative dispatch of 14 April 1831, and his request for Sturt's promotion, had had no result, and nothing came of the request by Sir Richard Bourke (who had succeeded Darling) that Viscount Goderich should give 'this deserving officer your Lordship's protection and support'. Though it seems to have been impossible to persuade the Colonial Office of the value of Sturt's work, his book had one important effect: it was read by Edward Gibbon Wakefield, and led to the choice of South Australia for the new settlement then in contemplation.

In May 1834, in view of his services, Sturt applied for a grant of land in Australia, intending to settle on it; and in July instructions were given that he was to receive a grant of 5,000 acres (2,000 ha). Sturt, on his part, agreed to give up his pension rights. On 20 September 1834, Sturt married Charlotte Christiana Greene, daughter of an old family friend, and soon afterward sailed for Australia.

Sturt returned to Australia in mid-1835 to begin farming on the 5,000 acres of land which had been granted to him by the New

South Wales Government. The property was on the lower reaches of Ginninderra Creek, near present-day Canberra, and Sturt named it Belconnen, a name now applied to the nearby population centre. In 1838, together with Giles Strangways, a Mr McLeod and Captain John Finnis, he herded 400 cattle overland from Sydney to Adelaide, on the way proving that the Hume and the Murray were the same river.

In September 1838 he led an expedition to the Murray mouth, and settled all dispute as to the suitability of Adelaide for the colony's capital. After returning to NSW to settle his affairs, Sturt settled at Grange, South Australia, in early 1839; he was appointed Surveyor General of South Australia and member of the South Australian Legislative Council, until the London-appointed Surveyor-General, Edward Frome, unexpectedly arrived. In the meantime, in December 1839, Sturt and his wife accompanied George Gawler, Julia Gawler, Henry Bryan and Henry Inman on a Murray River expedition, and visited Mount Bryan. Julia Gawler, Charlotte Sturt, and Charlotte's maidservant thereby became the first white women to travel the Murray. Sturt was briefly the Registrar-General, but he soon proposed a major expedition into the interior of Australia as a way of restoring his reputation in the colony and London.

In September 1841, Sturt chaired a Bench of Magistrates that conducted an official inquiry into the circumstances of the Rufus River massacre. The inquiry concluded 'that the conduct of Mr Moorhouse and his party was justifiable, and indeed unavoidable in their circumstances'.

Sturt was driven by a conviction that it was his destiny to discover a great salt-water lake, known as 'the inland sea', in the middle of Australia. At the very least, he wanted to be the first explorer to plant his foot in 'the centre' of Australia. In August 1844, he set out with a party of 15 men, 200 sheep, six drays and a boat, to explore north-western New South Wales and to advance into central Australia. They travelled along the Murray River and Darling River before passing the future site of Broken Hill, but then were stranded for months by the extreme summer conditions near the present site of Milparinka. When the rains eventually came, Sturt moved north and established a depot at Fort Grey in today's Sturt National Park. With a small group of men, including explorer John McDouall Stuart as his draughtsman, Sturt pressed on across Sturt's Stony Desert and into the Simpson Desert, but he was unable to go further and turned back to the depot. Sturt made a second attempt to reach the centre of Australia, but he developed scurvy in the extreme conditions. His health broke down and he was forced to abandon the attempt. John Harris Browne, surgeon on the expedition, assisted Sturt, took over leadership of the party, and after travelling 3,000 miles (4,800 km) brought it back to safety.

Early in 1847 Sturt went to England on leave. He arrived in October and was presented with the Royal Geographical Society's Gold Medal. He prepared his *Narrative of an Expedition into Central Australia* for publication, but it was not published until early in 1849. Throughout this time, he again suffered with poor eyesight.

Sturt returned to Adelaide with his family, arriving back in August 1849. He was immediately appointed Colonial Secretary, with a seat in the Council. There was no lack of work in the ensuing years. Roads were constructed, and navigation on the Murray was encouraged. But Sturt had renewed trouble with his eyes.

On 30 December 1851 Sturt resigned his position, was given a pension of £600 a year, and settled down on 500 acres of land close to Adelaide and the sea. But gold discoveries had increased the cost of living, and on 19 March 1853 Sturt and his family sailed for England. Sturt lived at Cheltenham and devoted himself to the education of his children.

In 1855, Sturt applied unsuccessfully for the position of Governor of Victoria and in 1858 for that of Governor of Queensland. Sturt's age, uncertain health, and comparatively small income were against him. By 1860 his three sons were all in the army, and the remainder of his family went to live at Dinan to economise after the expenses of education and fitting out. Unfortunately, the town was unhealthy and in 1863 they returned to Cheltenham. In 1864 Sturt suffered great grief from the death of one of his sons in India. In March 1869 he attended the inaugural dinner of the Colonial Society, at which Lord Granville mentioned that it was the intention of the Government to extend the Order of St Michael and St George to the colonies. Sturt allowed himself to be persuaded by his friends to apply for a knighthood (KCMG), but afterwards regretted he had done so when he heard there were innumerable applications.

Sturt's health had been very variable, and on 16 June 1869 he died suddenly. He was survived by his widow, two sons, Colonel Napier George Sturt, RE, and Major-General Charles Sheppey Sturt, and daughter Charlotte. Mrs Sturt was granted a civil list pension of £80 a year, and the Queen granted her the title of Lady Sturt as if her husband's nomination to a knighthood of the order of St Michael and St George had been gazetted. Reproductions of portraits by Crossland and Koberwein will be found in Mrs NG Sturt's Life, which suggest the charm and refinement of Sturt's character.

Sturt's life is summarised in the Australian Dictionary of Biography as follows:

Although Sturt probably entered his career as an explorer through influence, his selection was justified by results. He was a careful and accurate observer and an intelligent interpreter of what he saw, and it was unfortunate that much of his work revealed nothing but desolation. He prided himself with some justice on his impeccable treatment of the Aboriginals, and earned the respect and liking of his men by his courtesy and care for their well-being. Indeed his capacity for arousing and retaining affection was remarkable; it made him an ideal family man but a failure in public life. Without toughness and egocentricity to balance his poor judgment and business capacity he had little chance of success in colonial politics. In this sphere he might well be described as a born loser. He remained throughout his life an English Tory gentleman with an unshakeable faith in God. Sturt is buried in Cheltenham Cemetery, Gloucestershire.

EDWARD GIBBON WAKEFIELD 1796–1862

AUTHOR OF THE SOUTH AUSTRALIA
COLONY PRINCIPLES

Edward Gibbon Wakefield was the man with the greatest role in the foundation of South Australia. Wakefield was born to Quaker parents and educated at Westminster School. He was Secretary to the British Envoy in Turin in 1814, and eloped with an heiress named Eliza in 1816. She died in 1820 and he then abducted a 15-year-old heiress, which landed him in gaol for three years.

In Newgate Prison Wakefield studied systematic colonisation, and published *Sketch of a Proposal for Colonizing Australia* in 1829. His concept was based on civil liberty, social opportunity and equality for all religions. The sale of land was to finance immigration of labourers from Britain and the establishment of agricultural villages.

Torrens and Hindmarsh credited him with the major role in the formation of the South Australia Company, but Gouger and Bacon submitted the first proposals to the UK Government. Wakefield helped his brother draft the bill for the South Australian Colonization Commission, and the first colonists arrived in South Australia in 1836. In 1837 the New Zealand Association was formed at Wakefield's home. In 1839 he sent the first batch of colonists to New Zealand, and in 1841 a Charter was granted for erecting the colony of New Zealand.

Wakefield was born in London in 1796, the eldest son of Edward Wakefield (1774–1854), a distinguished surveyor and land agent, and Susanna Crush (1767–1816). His grandmother, Priscilla Wakefield (1751–1832), was a popular author for the young, and one of the introducers of savings banks.

Wakefield was educated at Westminster School in London, and in Edinburgh. He served as a King's Messenger and carried diplomatic mail all over Europe during the later stages of the Napoleonic Wars, before and after the decisive Battle of Waterloo. In 1816, he eloped with a Miss Eliza Pattle and they were subsequently married in Edinburgh. It appears to have been a love match, but no doubt the fact that she was a wealthy heiress did 'sweeten the pot', as Edward received a marriage settlement of £70,000 (almost $10m in 2019 Australian dollars), with the prospect of more when Eliza turned twenty-nine.

Accompanied by the bride's mother and various servants, the married couple moved to Genoa, where Wakefield was again employed in a diplomatic capacity. Here, his first child, Susan Priscilla Wakefield known as Nina, was born in 1817. The household returned to London in 1820 and a second child, Edward Jerningham Wakefield, was born. Four days later Eliza died, and Edward resigned his post. The two children were brought up by their aunt, Wakefield's older sister, Catherine.

Nina suffered from tuberculosis, and Wakefield took his daughter to Lisbon in Portugal in the hope of recovery. He employed a young peasant girl, Leocadia de Oliveira, to help care for Nina, and later fostered her. After Nina's death in 1835, Wakefield sent Leocadia on to Wellington, New Zealand, where she met John Taine and had 13 children.

Although wealthy by contemporary standards, Wakefield was not satisfied. He wished to acquire an estate and enter Parliament, and for this he needed more capital. He almost managed to wed yet another wealthy heiress in 1826 when he abducted 15-year-old Ellen Turner, after luring her from school with a false message about her mother's health. In 1827 Wakefield was brought to trial for the case, which was known as the Shrigley abduction, and along with his brother William, he was sentenced to three years in Newgate prison. The marriage had not been consummated and was dissolved by a special Act of Parliament. He then attempted to overturn his father-in-law's will and gain control of the remainder of his dead wife's money. This did not work either. In fact, the entire affair did a lot to tarnish his reputation, as there were strong suspicions that in order to strengthen his case he had resorted to forgery and perjury, although he was never tried for these.

Probably considering emigration upon his release, while he was in prison he turned his attention to colonial subjects; he considered the main causes of the slow progress of the Australian colonies, the enormous size of the landed estates, the reckless manner in which land was given away, the absence of all systematic effort at colonisation, and the consequent discouragement of immigration and dearth of labour. He proposed to remedy this state of things by the sale of land in small quantities at a sufficient price, and the employment of the proceeds as a fund for promoting immigration. These views were expressed in his *Letter from Sydney* (1829), which was published while he was still in prison but often quoted as if written in that colony.

After his release Wakefield briefly turned his attention to social questions at home. He produced a tract on the *Punishment of Death*, with a graphic picture of the condemned sermon in Newgate, and another on the rural districts, with an equally powerful exhibition of the degraded condition of the agricultural labourer. He soon, however, became entirely engrossed with colonial affairs.

In 1831, having impressed John Stuart Mill, Robert Torrens and other leading economists with the value of his ideas, Wakefield became involved in various schemes to promote the colonisation of South Australia. He believed that many of the social problems in Britain were caused by overcrowding and overpopulation, and he saw emigration to the colonies as a useful safety valve. He set out to design a good colonisation scheme, one with a workable combination of labourers, artisans and capital. The scheme was to be financed by the sale of land to the capitalists who would thereby support the other classes of emigrants.

It took several attempts to get the South Australian colony going. Although Wakefield was initially a driving force, he found that as it came closer to reality he was allowed less and less influence. Eventually he was frozen out almost completely, whereupon he took offence and severed his connections with the scheme. It was during this period that his daughter, Nina, died; and their time in Lisbon also meant that he was away from the scene of negotiations for several months. Nonetheless, in 1839 John Hill named the Wakefield River, a river north of Adelaide in South Australia, after Edward Gibbon Wakefield. This also led to the later naming of Port Wakefield.

However, he did not lose interest in colonisation as a tool for social engineering. In 1833 he anonymously published *England and America*, a work primarily intended to develop his own colonial theory, which is done in the appendix entitled *The Art of Colonization*. However, the body of the work contains many new ideas, some of them reaching apparently extreme conclusions. It contains the distinct proposal that the transport of letters should be wholly free, and the prediction that, under given circumstances, the Americans would raise 'cheaper corn than has ever yet been raised'.

Soon, a new project was under way: the New Zealand Association. In 1837 the Colonial Office gave the New Zealand Association a charter to promote settlement in New Zealand. However, they attached conditions that were unacceptable to the members of the Association. After considerable discussion, interest in the project waned. Wakefield was undoubtedly one of the most influential voices in the Association and he had discovered another interest - Canada.

The 1837 Rebellion in Lower Canada had been suppressed, but the colony was in turmoil. The Government of Lord Melbourne wanted to send John George Lambton, Lord Durham, to settle the disputes. He and Wakefield had been working together closely on the New

Zealand scheme, and he was a convert to Wakefield's colonial theories; the report embodied Wakefield's ideas, and he surreptitiously leaked it to *The Times*, to prevent the government from tampering with it. Durham was only prepared to accept the task if Wakefield accompanied him as Commissioner of Crown Lands. However, they both knew that Wakefield would be completely unacceptable to the British Government, so Durham planned to announce the appointment only after he had reached Canada. Wakefield and his son, Edward Jerningham Wakefield, sailed secretly for Canada in 1838, but before they arrived word had leaked out and the appointment was forbidden by London.

Despite this, Durham retained him as an unofficial representative, adviser and negotiator, giving him effectively the same powers he would have had if he been appointed. Between them they successfully defused the situation and brought about the union of Upper and Lower Canada. Since Durham was ill for much of his time in Canada, a great deal of the credit for the success of his mission belongs to his advisers, Wakefield and Charles Buller. Clearly, Wakefield had become a capable negotiator. Shortly afterwards, political manoeuvring in London made Durham's position untenable; he resigned and they all returned to Britain.

Durham went into seclusion while he wrote and then presented to Parliament a report on his administration. Although their names are not mentioned, it seems likely that report was written cooperatively by Durham, Buller and Wakefield. Eventually this report and its conclusions became a blueprint for development of British colonial policy.

The defunct New Zealand Association re-formed itself as the New Zealand Company in June 1838. By the end of the year they had purchased a ship, the *Tory*. Early in 1839 they discovered that although they now complied with the conditions the Government had laid down for the old New Zealand Association, the Government was not prepared to honour its promises. Furthermore, it was actively considering making New Zealand a British Colony, in which case land sales would become a government monopoly.

At a meeting in March 1839, Wakefield was invited to become the Director of the New Zealand Company. His philosophy was the same as when he planned his elopements: 'Possess yourself of the Soil and you are Secure'.

It was decided that the *Tory* would sail for New Zealand as soon as possible. Wakefield's brother William was appointed leader of the expedition, with his son Jerningham as his nominal Secretary. They had some difficulty finding a suitable captain for the *Tory*, but then found Edward Main Chaffers, who had been sailing master on *HMS Beagle* during Fitzroy's circumnavigation of the globe. Dr Ernst Dieffenbach was appointed as Scientific Officer, and Charles Heaphy as a draughtsman. The *Tory* left London on 5 May and called at Plymouth to complete the fitting out. Fearing a last-minute attempt by the Government to prevent her sailing, Wakefield hastened down to Plymouth and advised their immediate departure. The *Tory* finally quit English shores on 12 May 1839, and reached New Zealand ninety-six days later.

Wakefield did not sail with the colonists, and many years were to pass before he saw New Zealand. He probably also recognised that he did not have the patience, the skills or the talents needed on a frontier. His talents lay in visualising dramatic plans and grandiose schemes and then persuading other people to get involved. He was not even a good organiser, as he tended to ignore the details. He was a salesman, a propagandist and a politician, and secretly inspired and guided many Parliamentary Committees on colonial subjects, especially on the abolition of penal transportation. By the end of 1839 he had dispatched eight more ships to New Zealand, before he even knew of the success of the *Tory* expedition led by his brother William. He then recruited his brother, Arthur, to lead another expedition, this time to settle in the Nelson area at the top of the South Island. The 16-year-old son of his sister Catherine, Charles Torlesse, and the rector of Stoke-by-Nayland in Suffolk (who subsequently also went to New Zealand for a time), sailed with Arthur as a trainee surveyor. By now William's daughter, Emily, and his ward, Leocadia, were already in New Zealand. Two more of his brothers also eventually went to New Zealand, along with numerous nieces and nephews.

While active with the New Zealand Company, Wakefield had maintained his interest in Canadian affairs. He was involved with the North American Colonial Association of Ireland (NACAI). At his instigation, the NACAI were trying to purchase a large estate just outside Montreal, where they wanted to establish another colonial settlement. Wakefield pushed the scheme with his usual energy; apparently, the Government did not object in principle, but they strenuously objected to Wakefield having any part of it.

However, trusted or not by the politicians, Wakefield was involved in the scheme. The NACAI sent him back to Canada as their representative; he arrived in Montreal in January 1842 and stayed in Canada for about a year. At this stage, Canada was still coming to terms with the union of Upper and Lower Canada. There were serious differences between the French and English Canadians, with the English Canadians holding the political clout. Wakefield skilfully manipulated these differences and it was fairly easy for him to get the support of the French Canadians. By the end of that year he got himself elected to the Canadian Parliament. It is perhaps typical of Wakefield that, having been elected, he immediately returned to Britain and never took up his seat.

He returned to Canada in 1843 and spent some months there. However, when he heard of his brother Arthur's death at the Wairau Affray, he immediately quit Canada and never returned. This appears to be the end of his involvement with Canadian affairs, except that he was paid about £20,000 by the NACAI for his work in Canada.

Wakefield returned to England in early 1844 to find the New Zealand Company under serious attack from the Colonial Office. As usual, he threw himself into the campaign to save his project. Then, in August 1844, he had a stroke, followed in later months by several other minor strokes, and he had to retire from the struggle. There is also a possibility that his mental health was not too sound in the succeeding months. His son Jerningham returned from New Zealand at about this time and was on hand to care for him. In August 1845, he went to France to recuperate and to give himself a complete break from New Zealand affairs. However, it did not serve his purpose and he returned to London two months later in a semi-invalid state. During his convalescence he wrote *A View of the Art of Colonization*, in the form of letters between a 'Statesman' and a 'Colonist'.

By January 1846 Wakefield was back to his scheming. By now Gladstone was Colonial Secretary. Wakefield approached him early in the New Year with a fairly radical plan that both the Government and the New Zealand Company should withdraw from New Zealand affairs and the colony should become self-governing. While it might have been a good idea, Wakefield wanted it accepted immediately, and became at first heated and then distressed when some months later, it was still being considered.

Then, during August 1846, he had another, potentially fatal, stroke. His friend, Charles Buller took up the negotiations. In May 1847 the British Government agreed to take over the debts of the New Zealand Company and to buy out their interests in the Colony. The directors accepted the offer with alacrity. Wakefield found he was powerless and unable to influence the decision, which did not please him. Following his 1846 stroke, Wakefield was cared for by his niece, Alice Mary Wakefield, until his death in Wellington, New Zealand, in 1862.

Then came another distraction. Without notice, his youngest brother Felix, who had been in Tasmania since the early 1830s, reappeared in England accompanied by eight of his children, having abandoned his wife and youngest child in Australia. Felix had no money and no prospects and was unable to provide for his family. Wakefield found him somewhere to live and farmed out the children among various relatives, but it was another year before his health was strong enough to take over the role of surrogate father, Felix being apparently unable to do anything for his family.

Meanwhile, Wakefield was getting involved in a new scheme. He was working with John Robert Godley to promote a new settlement in New Zealand, this one to be sponsored by the Church of England.

This plan matured to become the Canterbury Settlement. The first ship sailed from England in December 1849, with Robert Godley in command of the expedition. Jerningham Wakefield also sailed with them, his health and finances having been ruined by his dissipated lifestyle in London. Then the first immigrant ships sailed from Plymouth in September 1850, bound for Canterbury, and others followed.

In the same year, 1850, Wakefield co-founded the Colonial Reform Society with Charles Adderley, a landowner and Member of Parliament for North Staffordshire.

Brother Felix was causing problems back in Britain, and brought Wakefield a great deal of grief. Felix decided that settlement in New Zealand was the solution to all his problems. Wakefield reluctantly sponsored his passage to Canterbury, where he was allocated 100 acres of land (40 hectares) near Sumner. He and six of his children arrived in Lyttelton in November 1851. A short time later one of other settlers described him as 'the worst man we have in Canterbury'.

During 1851 and 1852, Wakefield continued to work for the Canterbury Association and also worked towards making New Zealand a self-governing colony. The New Zealand Constitution Act was passed on 30 June 1852. There was general satisfaction among New Zealanders about this, although they were less happy to discover that the new Government was to be saddled with the remaining debts of the defunct New Zealand Company.

Wakefield now decided that he had achieved everything he could in England. It was time to see the colony he felt he had created. He sailed from Plymouth in September 1852 knowing he would never return. His sister Catherine and her son Charley came to see him off. Then, at the last minute, his father appeared. Edward Wakefield was now 78 years old, and he and Wakefield had not spoken since the Ellen Turner abduction twenty-six years before. They were reconciled, and the elder Edward died two years later.

The ship arrived at Port Lyttelton on 2 February 1853. Wakefield had travelled with Henry Sewell, who had been Deputy Chairman and full-time Manager of the Canterbury Association. It seems likely that Wakefield expected to be welcomed as a founding father of the colony, and to be feted and immediately asked to assume leadership of the colony. However, colonisation had inevitably changed the perspectives of the people of Canterbury. Many of them felt they had been let down and cheated by the Association, and the two new arrivals were firmly linked in their minds with the broken promises and disappointments of the Association.

James Edward FitzGerald, who was one of the leaders of Canterbury, and who was elected as Superintendent of the Canterbury Province a few months later (in July 1853), declined to meet with Wakefield for some days; he was certainly unwilling to relinquish control to someone he probably saw as a tainted politician from London.

Within a very short time Wakefield was completely disenchanted with Canterbury. He claimed the citizens were far too parochial in their outlook; they were far more concerned with domestic issues than with national politics. Clearly they were not worthy of Edward Gibbon Wakefield, and after only one month he left Canterbury and sailed for Wellington.

There was enough political ferment in Wellington to satisfy even Wakefield. Governor George Grey had just proclaimed self-government for New Zealand, but it was a watered down version, significantly less 'self-government' than was described in the New Zealand Constitution Act of the year before. In his own way, George Grey was every bit as unscrupulous as Wakefield, and he had very firm ideas on what was good for New Zealand. They were not necessarily bad ideas, but they were different from Wakefield's. It seems likely that even before they met, both men knew they would clash.

When they arrived in Wellington, Wakefield declined to go ashore until he knew he was going to be properly received by the Governor. Grey promptly left town. Sewell went ashore and met with various dignitaries. Among them was Daniel Bell Wakefield, another of the brothers who had been in Wellington for some years practising law, and was Attorney General of the Province. He also managed to get an address of welcome for Wakefield, written by Isaac Featherston and signed by many of the citizens.

Wakefield went on the attack almost as soon as he landed. He took issue with George Grey on his policy on land sales. Grey was in favour of selling land very cheaply to encourage the flow of settlers. Wakefield wanted to keep the price of land high so that the growth of the colony could be financed by land sales, which was a fundamental tenet of his colonial theory. He and Sewell applied for an injunction to prevent the Commissioner of Crown Lands from selling any further lands under Governor Grey's regulations. The Crown Commissioner was Wakefield's second cousin, Francis Dillon Bell - early New Zealand really was a Wakefield family business!

Within a month of arriving in Wellington, Wakefield began a campaign in London to have him recalled, not knowing he had already applied to leave the colony. Meanwhile, Grey was in control. He responded to the attacks on him by questioning Wakefield's integrity, always an easy target. He particularly focussed on the generous fees that had been paid to Wakefield as a Director of the New Zealand Company at a time when it was reneging on its debts in New Zealand. This served to remind the people of Wellington just how badly they had been let down by the Company and how angry they felt about it. Wakefield managed to clear himself of the actual charges, but a great deal of dirt was thrown around.

Elections for the Provincial Councils and General Assembly, the national parliament, were scheduled for August 1853. Wakefield stood for the Hutt electorate, and to the surprise of some and the disappointment of others, he was elected to both the Provincial Council and the General Assembly.

The first sitting of the Provincial Assembly was in October 1853. Wakefield was not only the most senior member but also clearly the most experienced politically. However, the Assembly was controlled by the Constitutional Party led by Dr Isaac Featherston, and they had been heavily involved in the recent criticism of his integrity. Working in opposition, Wakefield probably made certain that the Provincial

Assembly became a working democracy rather than a Constitutional Party oligarchy. His wide knowledge of parliamentary law and custom ensured that the body of the Assembly could not be ignored by the ruling party.

Early in 1854, the town of Wellington held a Founder's Festival. Three hundred people attended, including sixty Māori and all the Wakefields. The principal toast of the evening was to 'the original founders of the Colony and Mr Edward Gibbon Wakefield'. Whatever the vicissitudes of the last few months, it confirmed Wakefield as one of the leading political figures of the colony, possibly the only one with enough stature to take on Governor Grey.

But Grey was gone and Colonel Robert Wynyard was acting as Governor. Wynyard opened the first New Zealand Parliament on 27 May 1855. Wakefield and James Fitzgerald immediately began manoeuvring for positions of influence, with Wakefield moving for Parliament to appoint its own responsible government (Ministers of the Crown). Wakefield took a position supporting Wynyard, while FitzGerald took an opposite tack. The dispute over responsible government dragged on. As a compromise, on 7 June Wynyard appointed James FitzGerald to the Executive Council. Wakefield was not asked to form a part of the Ministry.

By July, FitzGerald was in serious conflict with Wynyard and resigned. Wakefield was summoned to form a government but he refused to do so, and said that he would advise Wynyard, so long as he acted on his advice alone. In effect, he sought to turn Wynyard into his own puppet. However, he did not have a majority of supporters in the house, and the Assembly was paralysed. It was prorogued by Wynyard on 17 August, but he had to recall it again by the end of the month, when he needed money to run the country. The new Ministry was composed mainly of Wakefield's supporters and it was soon clear that he was its de facto head. However, they failed to survive an early vote of no confidence, and New Zealand's second government collapsed. FitzGerald and his team returned to office. In the remaining two weeks of the Assembly's life they managed to pass some useful legislation before they were dismissed and new elections called.

Wakefield began electioneering in grand style. He was always able to move people with his speeches. He held two election meetings for his constituents in the Hutt Valley, which were well received. A third meeting was scheduled but never happened. On the night of the fifth of December 1855, Wakefield fell ill with rheumatic fever and neuralgia and he retired to his house in Wellington. He retired from the Hutt seat on 15 September 1855 and also retired from all political activity, making no more public appearances. He lived for another seven years, but his political life was over.

Edward Gibbon Wakefield died in Wellington on 16 May 1862.

He is mentioned and criticised in Chapter 33 of Karl Marx's *Das Kapital* (Volume 1) and similarly in Henry George's *How to Help the Unemployed*.

By the turn of the twenty-first century, the direct descendants of the Wakefield family in New Zealand were: William Wakefield Lawrence Clague, resident in Kapiti; and descendants of Edward's sister, Catherine Gurney Wakefield, who married Charles Torlesse. A great-great-nephew of William and Edward Gibbon Wakefield, William Clague is the great-great-grandson of John Howard Wakefield, one of the original brothers. John Howard Wakefield spent most of his life in India and ended his days back in England, unlike his two better-known siblings.

PUBLICATIONS

How to Help the Unemployed, by Henry George in The North American Review, Volume 158, Issue 447, February 1894.

Adventure in New Zealand by Edward Jerningham Wakefield, John Murray, 1845.

An Account of the Settlements of the New Zealand Company by The Hon HW Petre, Smith, Elder and Co, 1842.

A View of the Art of Colonization by Edward Gibbon Wakefield, 1849.

The Modern Theory of Colonisation last chapter in Karl Marx's *Capital, Vol I* focussed on Wakefield's theory.

Facts Relating to the Punishment of Death in the Metropolis by Edward Gibbon Wakefield, James Ridgway, 1831.

PASTOR KAVEL 1798-1860

LEADER, GERMAN IMMIGRANTS
TO SOUTH AUSTRALIA

Pastor Kavel arranged the first migration of Germans to Australia in 1838. They proved to be industrious and became highly successful in their new home, establishing the first wine industry. Their settlement in the Barossa Valley is now world famous.

August Kavel was born in Berlin, the son of a tailor. His father was able to obtain a grammar school education for his very talented son, who attended the Gymnasium zum Grauen Kloster school and went on to study theology. In 1826, he was ordained and installed as the Pastor at the church in the village of Klemzig, near the city of Züllichau in what was then south-eastern Brandenburg in the German state of Prussia. Between 1798 and 1840, the Protestant churches in Prussia had been subjected to a number of changes, brought about by the decrees of King Frederick William III. These decrees were intended to unify the Lutheran and Reformed Churches into one Evangelical

Christian Church. By 1826 there was some opposition to the intentions of Frederick William. This escalated in 1830, when Frederick William announced a number of changes that outlawed the traditional rites of the churches and prescribed a form of worship which many Lutherans believed was against the Will of God. It was in this environment that dissent against the decrees of Frederick William arose.

Pastor Kavel was not initially one of this group, who had come to be known as the Old Lutherans. In 1829, Frederick William's revised edition of the worship agenda was released for voluntary usage in congregations, as was the first edition. Pastor Kavel used this worship order until 1834 when, influenced by the writings of Johann Gottfried Scheibel, he ceased to do so and joined the ranks of the dissenters. Kavel wrote to the King in January 1835, informing him that he would no longer use the worship agenda. On Easter Monday 1835, Kavel was removed from the ministry and was prohibited from practising as a pastor. His congregation were also prohibited from using the church premises or participating in any worship services presided over by suspended Pastors.

Pastor Kavel decided to lead his congregation in an exodus from Prussia to a place where they could worship in freedom. In early 1836, he travelled to Hamburg to enquire into the possibility of migrating to Russia or the United States, but neither of these options was possible. However, while in Hamburg, Kavel was informed of the possibility of migrating to Australia. He travelled to London, England, to meet with George Fife Angas, the Chairman of the South Australian Company, which was searching for emigrants to settle the land acquisitions it had in South Australia. Kavel was received favourably by Angas, who sent his Chief Clerk, Charles Flaxman, to Prussia to meet with Kavel's group and to prepare them for emigration. Kavel remained in London, ministering to the German community.

The congregation in Klemzig went through a number of setbacks in their application to emigrate. They required permission from the Government, but in 1837 they were informed that their request for emigration was denied. Representatives who were sent to appeal against the denial were arrested and imprisoned. It was only at the end of 1837 that the group was finally given permission to emigrate.

The migration was expensive, and George Fife Angas had lobbied the South Australian Company to provide funding for the Lutheran dissenters, arguing that the character of the people was the ideal type for the new settlement in South Australia. However, there were financial problems within the Company and the request by Angas, which had initially been approved, was now denied. Many of the Prussian migrants had also encountered financial hardship due to the extended emigration application process. A migration to Australia now appeared to be impossible.

George Angas decided to personally provide funding to Kavel and the Klemzig group. Four ships were chartered on their behalf: the *Prince George*, the *Bengalee*, the *Zebra* and the *Catharina*. On 8 July 1838, the *Prince George* and the *Bengalee* left Hamburg with about 250 of the emigrants. They travelled to Plymouth, where they picked up Pastor Kavel, and then continued on their journey until they arrived in Port Adelaide on 20 November 1838. The *Zebra* left in August 1838 with 187 on board, and arrived in Holdfast Bay on 28 December. Eleven people, six adults and five children, died on the trip. The *Catharina* left in September 1838 and arrived in January 1839. In all, these ships transported 596 migrants from Prussia to Australia.

As the leader of the group of immigrants, Pastor Kavel acted as a negotiator for securing land for the settlers. The new migrants rented 150 acres from George Angas and established their first settlement in Australia at Klemzig. Although there would have been employment for everyone in the burgeoning Adelaide, the Klemzig Lutherans insisted on staying together, and leased a plot of 144 acres about six kilometres north of Adelaide on the Torrens River. There they built a small village which they named in memory of their old home, Neu-Klemzig. The picturesque new settlement drew many favourable comments from the English-speaking colonists. A contemporary newspaper depicts the newcomers as being assiduous '... as an English bee at springtime.., (the men) weed, water, fish, milk, wash and build wooden houses... and the women were … just as industrious, busy baking bread, making butter, cooking and many other things… There is not one lazy soul. Even the children who are still too young to work, receive regular school lessons conducted by their never tiring, outstanding pastor'.

After the arrival of the third ship, the *Zebra*, the town Hahndorf was established, and a third settlement of the Prussian migrants was established by many of the passengers of the *Catharina* at Glen Osmond. One of Kavel's followers, Johann Friedrich Krummnow, taught the girls en route but was deemed 'not completely satisfactory and the community did not allow him to teach in Australia'.

On 23 and 24 May 1839, Kavel convened a meeting of the elders of the three villages, Klemzig, Hahndorf and Glen Osmond. At this meeting, the constitution of the new Australian Lutheran synod was adopted. At the following synodical gathering in 1840, a letter was drafted and subsequently sent to the 'Old Lutherans' in Prussia. Its purpose was to encourage others to emigrate and, most importantly, have a second pastor emigrate to Australia.

Pastor Kavel provided the main push for German settlement of the Barossa Valley. He felt the distance between the first settlements would erode their common cultural and religious bonds and he suggested that all Lutherans should move to the Barossa, where George Angus had offered to sell 200 acres to the Germans. His flock was not enthusiastic and Kavel abandoned his plan but kept the offer open for future purchases. A group from the third Lutheran ship took advantage of the offer.

On 28 October 1841, 224 Prussians arrived in Adelaide on the *Skjold*, among them Pastor Gotthard Fritzsche. This group formed the main part of the settlements at Lobethal and Bethanien. Krummnow was able to purchase land at Lobethal as he was now a naturalised English citizen, and the settlers provided him with funds to establish a community. Krummnow wanted the community to be based on his own principles of shared property and fervent prayer, but the Lobethal settlers rejected his vision and legally disputed his right to the land titles. In 1842, Langmeil was settled. Kavel remained in South Australia until his death.

JOHN RIDLEY 1806-1887

INVENTOR OF 'RIDLEY'S STRIPPER'

South Australia's early success owed a lot to agriculture. The siting of arable land alongside St Vincent Gulf and on Yorke Peninsula allowed transport of grain by ship, which gave South Australia an advantage over California in the world's wheat trade. Ridley's contribution was to eliminate the need for a large number of labourers to bring in the harvest.

Early colonial stagnation had been overcome by expansion beyond the Barossa Valley, discovery of copper at Kapunda and the Victorian gold rush, which opened up the market for farm goods and set up the route for gold export from Adelaide. This was not to last, but it led to considerable investment in land and the population doubled in ten years. When self-government began, wheat farmers were given priority over stockmen.

John Ridley was a miller, and when he arrived in South Australia in 1840 he took over the flour mill, installed the first steam engine in the state and also invested in the copper mine at Burra. Wheat, of course, had been domesticated thousands of years ago by eliminating the genes responsible for allowing the seed to drop after maturation, which allowed its collection at a later stage for conversion into flour; this required many labourers. In 1843 the wheat crop threatened to exceed the work force available to harvest it, and the Corn Exchange in South Australia offered 40 pounds for a model or plans for a mechanical reaper. Many were rejected in September. However, by October 1843 Ridley was testing his version, and in November the newspaper reported that further trials had 'established its success'. In 1845, seven machines had been produced, and by 1850 over 50 were operating and a number had been exported.

John Ridley, miller, inventor and preacher, was born on 26 May 1806 at West Boldon, near Sunderland, Durham, England, the son of John and Mary Ridley, who were cousins. His formal education was little more than that provided by a village school, but it was augmented by an insatiable love of books and a remarkable memory. Although baptised into the Church of England, he came early under the influence of Wesleyan Methodism. He began preaching at 18 and at 23 was a recognised local preacher in the Sunderland circuit. At 15, he took over the milling business that his mother had managed since his father's death in 1811. After his mother's death in 1835, he married Mary Pybus, the daughter of a boarding school proprietor at West Boldon.

In 1839 Ridley left for South Australia in the *Warrior* with his wife and two children; sadly, soon after they arrived, one of the children died after her clothes caught fire. He took over the flour mill of the South Australian Company, installed a Watt's Beam steam engine, and began growing wheat on land he bought at Hindmarsh. With shrewd foresight he predicted that the heavy spending of Governor George Gawler would bring depression and force colonists into rural production. When this happened, he let his Hindmarsh farm and, as he toured the settled districts in search of grain for his mill, made many more land purchases.

When a prize was offered in September 1843 for designs of harvesting machinery, Ridley did not compete because he was already building a reaper based on a woodcut in JC Loudon's *An Encyclopaedia of Agriculture* (3rd ed, London, 1835). When it was tested the following month, his machine failed. It was rebuilt with combs and beaters (instead of cutters) to sweep off the heads of wheat, then tried out on his tenant's crop. That version proved successful, reaping seventy acres (28 ha) in a week at five shillings an acre. The following year, he planned the manufacture and improvement of his harvesting machine; in 1845 he made seven, and within five years over fifty were operating in the province and others had been exported.

Although it was claimed that the machine was invented in principle by John Wrathall Bull, none disputed that Ridley was its first practical producer. In 1844 he was awarded a special prize by the Agricultural and Horticultural Society, and in 1858 he was thanked by the South Australian Parliament for a service that had helped to make possible the vast increase in wheat growing in the province. Ridley's returns from the harvesting machine were substantial but meagre compared with the dividends from his original shares in the Burra copper-mine, his flour mill and his land investments.

On 18 March 1853 he left for Europe with his family in the steamer *Melbourne* and after lengthy travel on the Continent, settled in England to devote his eccentric enthusiasm to invention and religion. At his own cost he had printed tens of thousands of copies of sermons and tracts that appealed to his principles and distributed them widely to grateful and ungrateful recipients. He was also an energetic lay preacher and made many gifts to evangelical churches and missions. Tall, spare and dignified, he was a venerable figure, particularly when his dark, abundant hair whitened with age. He died in London on 25 November 1887.

John Ridley's altruism and passion for practical improvement were sincere, and meant more to him than his own financial success. His self-reliance made him eschew government rewards in South Australia, where his memory is honoured by the Ridley Memorial Scholarship at Roseworthy Agricultural College, memorial gates to the Royal Agricultural and Horticultural Society's showground at Wayville, and the electoral district of Ridley.

MARY LEE 1821-1909

SUFFRAGIST

Mary Lee led the fight for women's suffrage in South Australia, and in 1894 South Australian women were not only able to vote but also to sit in the parliament – a world first.

Mary came to Adelaide in 1879 as a widow, with her daughter and son. Her son died the following year and she afterward pushed for political and social reform. She was Secretary to Rev JC Kirby's Social Purity Society, which successfully raised the age of consent to 16 (Criminal Law Consolidation Act, 1885). She inaugurated the South Australian Women's Suffrage League in 1888 under Sir Edward Stirling's presidency, and adopted the reformist ideas of the Primitive Methodist, Rev Hugh Gilmore. Mary founded the Women's Trade Union in 1890 and was Secretary for two years.

In 1893 she presented to the Legislative Assembly a petition for female suffrage that was 400 feet long and contained 11,600 signatures. On 18th December 1894, the Constitution Amendment Act was passed, giving women the vote and allowing them a seat in Parliament. Conservatives had deliberately added the right for women to sit in Parliament in order to scotch the bill, but this backfired spectacularly. Although women had first been given the vote in September 1893 in New Zealand, their right to a seat in Parliament was unique to South Australia.

Mary Lee was born on 14 February 1821 in Monaghan, Ireland, the daughter of John Walsh. In 1844 she married George Lee, organist and vicar-choral of Armagh Cathedral; they had four sons and three daughters. In 1879 Mary, widowed, sailed for Adelaide with her daughter Evelyn, to nurse her sick son, John Benjamin; after his death the following year, they remained there, as Mary was becoming devoted to 'dear Adelaide', and could not in any case afford to leave.

For the rest of her life, Mary Lee, 'once the slip of an old red-hot Tory stem', worked single-mindedly for political and social reform. Her qualities of leadership, conviction and perseverance matched the social and political climate of late nineteenth-century South Australia. Initially interested in Jewish colonisation, Mary later became the Ladies' Secretary of Rev JC Kirby's Social Purity Society, which was working for legal changes in women's sexual and social status. Through the society's intensive lobbying and its stimulus of public and parliamentary debate, substantial alterations - including raising the age of consent to sixteen - were incorporated in the Criminal Law Consolidation Amendment Act (1885). Kirby gave Lee the principal credit for this.

She and other Purity Society members, recognising that women's suffrage was essential to their further improved status, inaugurated the South Australian Women's Suffrage League in July 1888. Through her work in the League, initially as Co-Secretary and soon after as Secretary, Mary Lee played a major part in South Australian political history. She saw the suffrage as her 'crowning task' and, under Sir Edward Stirling's presidency, steered the campaign skilfully, combining her experience of political processes with her knowledge of women's social disabilities and of the value of publicity in awakening public interest and understanding.

Unafraid of controversy, determined and sometimes abrasive, Mary Lee publicised her commitment in the *Register*:

If I die before it is achieved, like Mary Tudor and Calais, 'Women's enfranchisement' shall be found engraved upon my heart.

She regarded men's suffrage as 'only half a victory' and female suffrage as 'the pivot on which turns the whole question of the moral, social and industrial status of women'. From July 1888, the League's objects remained simply the enfranchisement of women on equal terms with men, without claiming access to parliamentary seats. From 1891 Lee worked harmoniously with the League's second President, Lady Colton, and Stirling and Catherine Helen Spence became Vice-Presidents.

In frequent speeches, newspaper articles and letters, Mary Lee illustrated her case by using historical, literary and biblical allusions; this did not prevent the 'abuse' and 'obloquy' of opponents, most of whom argued on traditional grounds against women voting. Short, plump and erect, she went energetically about the city, suburbs and country, speaking eloquently at League meetings and socials, at Democratic clubs and, despite her dislike of total abstinence, at Woman's Christian Temperance Union meetings. She planned the League's wider strategies and also collected shilling subscriptions and organised petitions and deputations. A practical Christian, she had adopted the social reformist ideas of the Primitive Methodist minister, Hugh Gilmore.

Acting on her concern at working women's conditions, and simultaneously promoting the suffrage cause, she proposed the formation of women's trade unions at a public meeting on sweatshops in December 1889. The Working Women's Trades Union was founded the following year, and she was its Secretary for two years; her visits to clothing factories and workshops, to persuade employers to adopt the union's log of prices, met with some success. In 1893, as the Union's Vice-President, she was their delegate to the Trades and Labor Council. In that capacity, she worked with Augusta Zadowon on a sub-committee examining sweating in the clothing trades; and she also worked on the Distressed Women's and Children's Committee, which distributed relief clothes and food to women suffering in the economic depression. She was a member of the Ladies' Committee of the Female Refuge.

As a supporter of the single tax, Mary Lee responded fluently - proclaiming women's suffrage - to a toast to the ladies, at a farewell to Henry George in 1890. She corresponded with New Zealanders and with women in other colonies, notably Lady Windeyer in Sydney, whom she advised on organising the Womanhood Suffrage League of New South Wales on South Australian League principles, and Rose Scott.

In Parliament, Stirling's successful 1885 resolution for female suffrage was followed by seven suffrage bills from 1886; five of them had a property qualification and six failed to gain the required statutory majority. Lee joined League deputations to   Premiers Playford, Holder and Downer, and from 1889 she worked tirelessly on numerous parliamentary petitions. With United Labor Party backing from 1891, the issue was approaching realisation. Premier Kingston's Minister for Education presented a female suffrage bill in 1893, but an attached referendum condition caused its failure and Mary's patience snapped. One journalist deplored her hot temper when she called the Labor Party 'a lot of nincompoops'.

However, Kingston acknowledged public demand and political pressure for female suffrage, and his government presented an unencumbered bill in July 1894. Mary Lee organised the colony-wide petition with 11,600 signatures which was presented to the House of Assembly in August. Women 'deluged' members with telegrams and thronged the galleries; over fifty members spoke, flippantly or seriously. Finally, on 18 December 1894, the Constitution Amendment Act was passed, and South Australian women were the first in Australia to gain the parliamentary vote, on the same terms as men. The Act also gave them the right to postal votes and to stand for Parliament, which were unique provisions anywhere. Mary Lee was exhausted but jubilant, and received congratulatory letters from Kingston and Chief Secretary (Sir) JH Gordon.

In 1895 two trade unions nominated Mary Lee to stand for Parliament but she declined, preferring to work 'on the side of right … unfettered by pledge or obligation to any party whatever'. On her 75th birthday in 1896 at the Adelaide Town Hall, Kingston handed her a purse of fifty sovereigns, publicly donated through the Mary Lee Testimonial Fund, with a 'handsomely bound and artistically engrossed' address which acknowledged that the achievement of women's suffrage 'is mainly due to your persistent advocacy and unwearied exertions'. At public meetings before the March 1896 elections Lee advised women on their voting duties.

That year the Government appointed Mary Lee as the first female official visitor to the lunatic asylums, and she performed this task with courage and compassion for twelve years, visiting the Destitute Asylum regularly as a friend to the inmates. In 1898 she backed the Medical Superintendent on the contentious issue of Paris Nesbit's release from Parkside Lunatic Asylum, maintaining that special provision should be made for such brilliant and disturbed patients.

As her financial resources dwindled, Lee asked Sir Josiah Symon to arrange the sale of her library. In 1902 Kirby initiated an appeal for her relief in the *Express and Telegraph* and the *Australian Woman's Sphere*, but there was only a poor response. Kirby observed that although many had benefited from her work, her advanced views and outspokenness had not made her widely loved. She complained bitterly to Rose Scott that her public work had all been at her own expense. Although her daughter Evelyn worked in the Telegraph Department, Mary's last years were blighted by poverty. She died in her North Adelaide home on 18 September 1909 and was buried in the Wesleyan cemetery, Walkerville, with her son Ben. Her daughter and a son in England survived her. Her work remained unrecorded until 1980. Her only memorial is her tombstone, a small white marble scroll, engraved 'Late Hon. Sec. Women's Suffrage League of S.A.'.

CATHERINE HELEN SPENCE 1825–1910

SUFFRAGIST AND AUTHOR

Catherine Helen Spence was born on 31 October 1825 near Melrose, Scotland. She was a writer, preacher, reformer and feminist, and became Australia's 'Grand Old Lady of Letters'. Her portrait adorns the Federation five-dollar bank note.

She was the daughter of David Spence, lawyer and banker, and his wife Helen, née Brodie. When her father David's wheat speculations failed in 1839, Catherine could not further her education in Edinburgh. The family migrated to South Australia in the *Palmyra*, arriving in November. David Spence was Clerk to the first Adelaide Municipal Council from 1840-43.

In Adelaide, Catherine Helen Spence became a governess and set out to fulfil her childhood ambition to be 'a teacher first and a great writer afterwards'. Her first two novels were published anonymously. *Clara Morison: A Tale of South Australia During the Gold Fever*, was published in London in 1854 and was the first novel about Australia written by a woman. It was followed by *Tender and True: A Colonial Tale* in 1856. *Mr. Hogarth's Will* (1865) was the first to bear her name as author; then came *The Author's Daughter* (1868). *Gathered In* was serialised in the Adelaide *Observer* in 1881-82; and *Handfasted*, submitted for a prize offered by the *Sydney Mail* in about 1880, was rejected as 'calculated to loosen the marriage tie ... too socialistic and therefore dangerous', and was not published. Spence's works were never popular, but they were respected. As she grew older, her ambition changed and she stopped writing novels. *An Agnostic's Progress from the Known to the Unknown* (1884) and *A Week in the Future* (1889) were her last major works of fiction.

In her *Autobiography* (1910) she wrote, discerningly, 'my work on newspapers and reviews is more characteristic of me, and intrinsically better work than I have done in fiction'. By 1878 she had won repute as a literary critic and social commentator, with articles in South Australian newspapers, the *Cornhill Magazine*, *Fortnightly Review* and *Melbourne Review*. As a regular, paid contributor to the *South Australian Register*, she was able to express her keen interest in the colony and its future, and she obtained a ready forum for her chosen causes.

In 1872 Spence helped Caroline Emily Clark to found the Boarding-Out Society, with the aim of boarding orphaned, destitute and reformed delinquent children in the homes of families, and visiting them to check on their behaviour and treatment. She was an official of the Society in 1872-86 and worked strenuously as a visitor. When the State Children's Council was established in 1886, she became a member, and was later a member of the Destitute Board.

Most of her work for education was done with her pen. Spence supported the foundation of kindergartens and a government secondary school for girls. In 1877 she was appointed to the School Board for East Torrens, an ineffectual and short-lived body. Her book *The Laws We Live Under* (1880) was the first social studies textbook used in Australian schools, and preceded similar courses in the other colonies by twenty years.

Spence had become an enthusiast for electoral reform in 1859 when she read JS Mill's review of Thomas Hare's system of proportional representation. In 1861 she wrote, printed (at her brother's expense) and distributed *A Plea for Pure Democracy. Mr. Hare's Reform Bill Applied to South Australia*; but she commented that 'it did not set the Torrens on fire'. She later claimed that Hare's system had been her life's major cause, but she ignored it between 1861 and 1892, except to inject a discussion of it into *Mr. Hogarth's Will*, and she paid a visit to Hare during a holiday in Britain in 1864-65. She had initially presented Hare's scheme as a means of ensuring representation of minorities by men of virtue, learning and intelligence, which was seen as conservative support of privilege. In 1892 she propounded the modified Hare-Spence system as the only way of attaining truly proportionate representation of political parties, an argument well suited to the current political climate of the colony.

By then Spence had acquired greater confidence. She became an accomplished public speaker, a process that had begun when she was the first woman to read papers to the South Australian Institute, and it brought her acclaim when she addressed the Australasian conferences on charity in 1891 and 1892. In about 1856, after much doubt and distress over the doctrines of the Church of Scotland in which she had been raised, she joined the Unitarian Christian Church. In 1878 she substituted for the minister and read a published sermon, and in the same year she delivered one of her own. Later she frequently preached in Adelaide, and occasionally in Melbourne and Sydney.

R Barr Smith gave financial backing for her campaign for proportional representation; it was supported by the nascent Labor Party and several small populist and socialist groups, and was launched with widespread public meetings in 1892–93. This was to avoid 'first past the post' systems requiring a 'runoff' vote and to give voters greater discrimination if their first choice did not win. In 1893 Spence went to the Chicago World Fair to address the International Conference on Charities and Correction, the Proportional Representation Congress, the Single Tax Conference, the Peace Conference, and a gathering in the Women's Building. She then lectured and preached across the United States, visited Britain and Switzerland and returned to South Australia in 1894. In the following year she formed the Effective Voting League of South Australia. She ran for the Federal Convention in 1897 – Australia's first female political candidate – and came twenty-second out of thirty-three candidates. In 1899 and 1900 she campaigned unsuccessfully for the introduction of 'effective voting' in Federal elections, and in 1902–1910 her supporters introduced proportional representation bills into the South Australian parliament. The heterogeneous executive of her Effective Voting League exemplified her non-party and probably personal following. Spence was 67 when she began her campaign, white-haired, short, stout, energetic, with a 'carrying' but not strident Scot's burr, and a direct, natural, sometimes brusque manner. She aroused much enthusiasm, especially for herself as a woman transcending social restrictions on permissible activities.

Spence joined the fight for female suffrage in 1891 and became a Vice-President of the Women's Suffrage League of South Australia. After South Australian women were enfranchised in 1894, she supported campaigns in New South Wales and Victoria and spoke at meetings of the Woman's League, a body formed in Adelaide for the political education of women. She urged the establishment of a local organisation affiliated with the International Council of Women. This work also won her acclaim and she had become a symbol of what Australian women could attempt. When she died on 3 April 1910, she was mourned as 'The Grand Old Woman of Australia'. She had lived with her parents (her father died in 1843, her mother in 1886) and had raised three families of orphaned children in succession. Her estate was sworn at £215. Her portrait hangs in the South Australian Art Gallery.

GEORGE WOODROFFE 'BUD' GOYDER
1826–1898

DISCOVERER OF GOYDER'S LINE

Goyder was a surveyor in South Australia during the latter half of the nineteenth century and defined the geographical limits for successful crop farming in South Australia (popularly known as Goyder's Line). He was born in Liverpool, England, the son of Sarah and David George Goyder, the latter a Swedenborgian minister and physician. He moved to Glasgow with his family, where he worked with an engineering firm and studied surveying. In 1848, at the age of 22, Goyder followed his sister and brother-in-law, George Galbraith McLachlan, to Sydney. He spent time working with an auctioneering firm and moved to Adelaide in 1851, obtaining work as a civil service draftsman. He rose rapidly in the civil service, becoming Assistant Surveyor-General by 1856 and Surveyor-General by 1861.

Goyder is remembered today for Goyder's Line of rainfall, a line used in South Australia to demarcate land climatically suitable for arable farming from that suitable only for light grazing. He was also an avid researcher into the lands of South Australia (including the present-day Northern Territory) and made recommendations to a great number of settlers in the newly developing colony, especially to those exploiting the newly discovered mineral resources of the state.

He married Frances Mary Smith on 10 December 1851 at Christ Church, North Adelaide, and the couple had nine children. Frances died on 8 April 1870 and on 20 November 1871 George married her sister Ellen Priscilla Smith, who had been looking after the children. With Ellen, George had three children, a son and twin daughters.

Goyder led an austere and disciplined life, which was reflected in his strict treatment of subordinates. However, in spite of many complaints by farmers and graziers, he was always regarded as fair in his advice. By the late 1880s, his health was declining, and with no improvement in sight, he resigned the post of Surveyor-General at the end of 1893. He died at Warrakilla, his home at Mylor near Aldgate in the Adelaide Hills, on 2 November 1898 and was buried in the Stirling District Cemetery.

In his period as Assistant Surveyor-General Goyder made many expeditions into the outback regions of South Australia, thinking that the water in the lakes he saw was fresh and permanent, rather than exceedingly erratic. He wrote many letters to newly established pastoralists in the arid regions of the state's north, and also surveyed the budding mining industry in the Flinders Ranges.

His early years as Surveyor-General were very difficult, especially his efforts to help set up settlement in the Northern Territory by supervising the establishment of the pastoral leaseholds that continue to the present day. Pastoralists were hit by a major drought in the middle of the decade and many were forced to move away from their cattle stations by the end of 1865. Goyder was also faced with the despair of his first wife, who suffered the loss of twins at birth during his long travels in the outback. Goyder resigned his position as Surveyor-General in 1894, completing a public service career that spanned 41 years.

Goyder provided advice about the geographic limits of crop growing in South Australia. Before the drought of the mid-1860s, wheat and barley growing had been spreading rapidly further north and the erroneous belief that rain would 'follow the plough' (also held in America) led to the idea of cereal crops spreading up to the Northern Territory border. However, the 1864–65 drought put paid, at least temporarily, to these ambitions. In the midst of his work in the pastoral zone, Goyder was asked to do a report on the problem and his response was to find out how far south crop failure had been general. The idea was to define the areas which deserved drought relief, but this gradually evolved into a demarcation between arable land and that more suitable for pasture. The northernmost point at which crops had not failed was marked as 'Goyder's Line of Rainfall' and corresponds approximately to the 300-millimetre (12-inch) annual isohyet (figures vary from 250 to 350 millimetres in different publications). Goyder recommended that farmers not attempt to farm cereal crops anywhere north of this line. The idea was quite contrary to beliefs widespread at the time and seen as ridiculous by many people in high places. Crops in the northern areas were excellent from 1872 to 1874 and nearly 250,000 new acres in wheat were the result. A Melbourne reporter described the 'land panic' which ensued. Expansion continued, but the droughts of 1880-1882 put paid to the earlier exuberance. In the 140 years since then, the many major droughts have proven that Goyder's advice was very wise, as they have led to major losses by all grain-growers near to, or north of, the line.

Goyder is otherwise remembered for the siting, planning and initial development of Darwin, the Northern Territory capital and principal population centre. After Finniss's recommendation of a site at Escape Cliffs was rejected, the current site was chosen for its exceptionally good water supply and potential for easy communication with the rest of the continent through land or sea transportation. Goyder was sent by the Government of South Australia (which included the Territory at that time) to lay out the street plans for a capital to be named Palmerston. With the incentive of a £3,000 bonus, 'Little Energy' - as he was nicknamed - and his team of around 128 men left Port Adelaide on the *Moonta* around 26 December 1868, and dropped anchor in Darwin Harbour on 5 February 1869. He selected the site on Fort Point near Port Darwin, and nearby townships to be named Daly, Southport and Virginia. They began the work in 1869, and completed all four in 18 months. Goyder returned on the *Gulnare* to Adelaide in November 1869 with around thirty men, and the greater part of his party returned in October 1870, although many (Dr Robert Peel, George MacLachlan, John Packard, Alfred and Frederick Schultze included) remained to fill positions in the town. Others, including Dan Daly and Paul Foelsche, returned within a few years.

Among the 100-odd members of Goyder's expedition were: GS Aldridge, JH Aldridge, GM Armstrong, J Austin, W Barlow, RW Barrow, Tom Bee, DR Beetson, JWO Bennett, M Bennett, Edwin S Berry, HS Bosworth, W Brooking, J Brooks, PH Burden, W Collett, Dan D Daly, H Edwards, W Fisher, Paul Foelsche, M Francis, JW Gepp, J Gerald, Christopher Giles, W Guy, W Hardy, William Harvey, R Hinton, W(illiam) Webster Hoare (assistant to Dr Peel), W Holland, RA Horn, TS Horn, W Howe Snr, CN Greene, G Hughes, G Kersley, S King, RR Knuckey, JM Lambell, C Laycock, J Loudon, RJ Loveday, AL McKay, George MacLachlan, Gilbert R. McMinn, AE Millaw, C Miller, WW Mills, AJ Mitchell, W Charles Musgrave, H Nottage, HD Packard, John H Packard, Dr R Peel, G Richards, J Le MF Roberts, W Rowe, Alfred Schultze, Frederick Schultze, AH Smith, EM Smith, C Spencely, CW Sprigg, AJ Thomas, JM Thomas, Charles Frederick Wells, and AT Woods, Ned and John Ryan (SA Govt Surveyors). Most are commemorated in the names of Darwin streets and outlying localities.

Soon afterwards, the Overland Telegraph was landed there from England (via present-day Indonesia) and it commenced operation in 1872. In 1911 Palmerston was renamed Darwin, but the name Palmerston was resurrected around 1980 for Darwin's satellite city to the south.

Goyder Road in Darwin is named for George Goyder, as are a large river in Arnhem Land and electorates in both the Northern Territory and South Australia. Mount Woodroffe, the highest peak in South Australia at 1,435 metres (4,710 ft) is named after him. Goyder's name has also been given to a species of grasswren (*Amytornis goyderi*, Gould 1875), a district council, an electorate, the new pavilion at the Royal Adelaide Showgrounds, several streets, a park and the Goyder Institute for Water Research.

WILLIAM BOOTHBY 1828-1903

CREATOR OF THE "AUSTRALIAN BALLOT"

Boothby made the electoral system in South Australia more efficient by introducing voting papers with a 'cross in the box' requirement, designing separate voting stalls for electors, and placing the votes in a sealed box. He also made the process more secure to minimise the possibility of bribery and corruption. His system, which was to be called the Australian Ballot, eventually spread to the United States and Europe.

William was the eldest son of South Australian Supreme Court Justice Benjamin Boothby. He was born at Nottingham, England, and in 1853, at the age of 24, emigrated to Australia with his parents. He had an MA from the University of London, where he likely read the works of political reformers like Jeremy Bentham and John Stuart Mill with their emphasis on making government more representative. He had also served as secretary in a local election in Yorkshire.

As many South Australians had left for the gold rush in Victoria, he easily found employment and in 1854 was appointed Deputy-Sheriff. In 1856 he was promoted to Sheriff just a few months before South Australia achieved responsible government. William was given the task of running the first elections under the new Constitution. The Government bore the cost of the elections as there were no established parties to sponsor them, and District Returning Officers were chosen to manage the votes and the rolls. The Legislative Council was designed as a single province and William was the first Provincial Returning Officer. He became a source of expert advice to the Government on electoral matters.

He prepared the clauses of the South Australian Act of 1856 that instituted voting by ballot, and the clauses of the Act of 1858 that provided for the placing of a cross against the name of the favoured candidate. Previously voters in the United Kingdom were given a list of candidates' names and voters crossed off those not in favour. Boothby based his reform on ballots pre-printed with the candidates' names. In a manner similar to that still used widely today, the voter marked the form in secret and placed it in a sealed box. William designated a number of separate tables where electors could have their names checked against the rolls, and individual booths where voters could mark their papers away from the view of other interested parties. This greatly speeded up the voting process and reduced waiting times. The ballots were collected and counted so that no one could be identified from their voting paper.

William also regularised the duties and payment of the District Returning Officers. At first these officers exercised some autonomy, but in 1896 the Provincial Returning Officer became their supervisor, setting up a clear chain of command. This was a precursor to the Chief Electoral Officer set up by the Commonwealth Electoral Act of 1902. As the Provincial Returning Officer, Boothby improved the management of the rolls. First, he recommended continuous rather than annual enrolment, giving the returning officers part-time work throughout the year. Then he established some co-ordination between government agencies, requiring the Registrar of Births, Deaths and Marriages to notify Returning Officers of electors' deaths, and instituted a system to transfer electors' names from one district to another when they moved. Following this it became the Government's job to compile the rolls instead of it being up to eligible voters to apply to have their names added. Boothby had local authorities deliver enrolment forms to every house in the colony – an impressive feat at the time. Voters had to fill in and return the forms and, on Boothby's advice, this was compulsory. There was no widespread objection to this compulsion, which showed the voters' respect for the Government of the day. Boothby's system was adopted for use in Federal government elections in Australia. In the second half of the 19th century, the use of the secret ballot spread to the United States and Europe; in 1892, Grover Cleveland became the first US President elected by Boothby's system, universally referred to as 'the Australian ballot' for nearly a century.

In the middle of the nineteenth century, South Australia developed the first permanent electoral administration in the world, overseen by a Chief Electoral Officer whose position and salary were set by legislation: Jeremy Bentham's *Election Master General* was realised in William Boothby.

Boothby suggested one more innovation: voting through the post as a cheap alternative for outlying districts. It was not taken up because the secret ballot was just beginning and it was feared the postal vote would reopen opportunities for bribery and corruption. South Australia did introduce limited postal voting in 1890 for outlying areas and absentee voters, with elaborate safeguards attached.

In 1893 Boothby was created a Companion of the Order of St Michael and St George (CMG). The Federal seat of Boothby, established in 1903 in Adelaide, was named in his honour. In his later years, he became Comptroller of Prison Labour and a Senator of the University of Adelaide in South Australia. He died in Adelaide.

PETER WAITE 1834-1922

EARLY SOUTH AUSTRALIAN
PASTORALIST AND PHILANTHROPIST

Peter Waite was a pioneer pastoralist and benefactor of the University of Adelaide. The Waite Research Institute, which contains the largest concentration of agricultural research and teaching expertise in the Southern Hemisphere, is named after him. He was born in Kirkcaldy, Scotland in 1834, the third son of James and Elizabeth Waite. His father died in the same year as a result of a fall from a horse, leaving his mother to carry on the modest family farm, Pitcairn, and raise their children, James, 5, David, 3, and Peter, 5 months. Peter undertook an apprenticeship in ironmongery, and worked in Edinburgh and Aberdeen.

In 1859 when he was 25 years old, Peter decided to join his brothers who had migrated to the Colony of South Australia. At the time he had been engaged for two years to his cousin Matilda Methuen and she agreed to wait until he was in a position to send for her. It is likely the

Waite brothers were influenced in their decision to migrate to South Australia by reports received through the family of merchant and ship-owner, George Elder, also from Kirkcaldy. Elder's sons had already established a successful family business in the new colony.

When he arrived in Adelaide in 1859, Peter joined his brother James at Pandappa, a pastoral property near Terowie in the north east of South Australia. He quickly adapted to the harsh conditions and in 1862 Thomas Elder offered him the lease of a nearby property, Paratoo. In 1863, James Waite was drowned while crossing a flooded creek on horseback, and Peter took over both stations.

By 1864, Peter had established himself as a pastoralist and property manager, and the Paratoo homestead had been made comfortable. He was now in a position to send for his fiancée, Matilda. She sailed for South Australia on the maiden voyage of the *City of Adelaide* and their marriage took place at Robert Barr Smith's home at Woodville in November 1864. Then followed a long journey for the newlyweds to Paratoo, in horse-drawn vehicles.

Peter Waite was innovative in his improvement and management of the semi-arid salt bush country. He set up fenced paddocks, imported 265 tons of fencing wire, and designed a metal dropper to support the fences. He sank wells and bores, and experimented with the use of steam traction engines for the excavation of earth tanks known as dams. His aim was for each paddock to have as permanent a supply of water as possible, and to rotate the sheep between paddocks. Peter was a strong advocate of 'spelling', where pastures were periodically spelled, or protected from grazing, to allow for their regeneration. It was estimated that by 1874, only 15 years after his arrival in the colony, he was overseeing a large area carrying 260,000 sheep.

In the 1860s and 1870s, Thomas Elder, NE Phillipson and Peter Waite acquired further leases to the east and north of Paratoo, an area which was largely undeveloped at that time. The Beltana Pastoral Company was initiated in 1862 by Thomas Elder, and Peter Waite supervised it from 1869; it ultimately comprised many runs stretching from the Flinders Ranges to the South Australia-Queensland border.

The lease of Mutooroo was acquired in 1868. After Sir Thomas Elder died in 1897, Robert Barr Smith became Chairman of the Board of Directors of the Beltana Pastoral Co Ltd and the Mutooroo Pastoral Co Ltd. Waite became the Managing Director of these companies, frequently visiting their landholdings to check on operations.

Peter Waite was a member and Vice-President of the Pastoralists Association of South Australia and West Darling, and the Federated Employers' Council of South Australia. In 1875 he became Chairman of the Stockbreeders' Association.

By 1874 Peter Waite was a Justice of the Peace and resident magistrate at Paratoo. His career continued to expand rapidly on all fronts - financial, commercial, domestic and social.

While visiting Adelaide in the early 1870s Peter expressed interest in a 54-hectare property at Urrbrae. In 1875 Thomas Elder helped Peter to acquire the property, with the understanding that Elder might agist his racehorses there. In 1875 the Waite family moved from Paratoo to a rented residence at Glenelg before finally moving into Urrbrae House in 1877 on their return from an overseas visit.

In the late 1880s a major reconstruction and enlargement of Urrbrae House was undertaken; when completed in 1891, it was one of Adelaide's significant mansions. Peter took a great interest in the décor of the House, employing Aldam Heaton from London to advise on the furnishings. In 1891 Urrbrae House was the first home in Adelaide to have electric lighting and it also had a refrigeration system installed in 1895.

Peter Waite had an interest in the arts and built a collection of contemporary watercolours, including some purchased in Rome as well as 31 paintings from Arthur Streeton. He was a member of the Adelaide Hunt Club and a hunting horn featured on the family crest. The motto on the crest, *Fac et Spera* ('Do and Hope') best represents his full and enthusiastic life.

Over the years Peter Waite became increasingly involved with the administration of Thomas Elder's companies. In 1883 he became Chairman of Elders Wool and Produce Co Ltd, which controlled the auction side of the wool and produce business. When this merged with the parent company in 1888, it became Elder Smith and Co Ltd, with Peter Waite as Chairman of Directors. Peter held this position for 33 years. He also had directorships in the Commercial Union Assurance Co Ltd, the British Broken Hill Co Ltd, and the SA Woollen Co Ltd.

Five children were born when Peter and Matilda were living at Paratoo Station. The couple's first child, Agnes, was born in 1866 in Burra. A son, James, was born in 1867, followed in 1869 by a second son, John, who lived only for 12 days. Matilda then travelled to Glenelg for the births of Elizabeth in 1870 and Lily in 1873. After the family moved to Adelaide, David was born in 1875. A seventh child, Maud, was born in 1877 but she lived only two months. The youngest daughter, Eva, was born in 1880. In 1879 Agnes died from complications following diphtheria.

Peter Waite's eldest son, James, did not follow in his father's pastoral footsteps but went to England in 1885 to train as an engineer, and had a distinguished career. James married in England and had one daughter, Peter Waite's only grandchild, Dorothy.

Peter Waite's third son David worked in the pastoral businesses in which his father was involved, and was well known in both pastoral and social circles in South Australia. While travelling by ship to the United Kingdom via South Africa in May 1913, he disappeared overnight. This was a tragic event for the Waite family, especially for his 79-year-old father.

In October 1913 Peter Waite wrote to the Premier of South Australia, Hon AH Peake, and the Chancellor of the University of Adelaide, the Rt Hon Sir Samuel Way, informing them that subject to his own and his wife's life interests, he intended presenting the Urrbrae property of 120 acres (54 hectares) to the University. The eastern half was to be used for scientific studies related to agriculture and the western half as a public park. He also intended handing over 45 hectares adjoining Urrbrae to the Government of South Australia for the purpose of establishing an agricultural high school. This statement of intent was subject to South Australian Parliament making the gifts free of succession duty.

In explaining his gift, Peter Waite wrote:

I have been much influenced by the wonderful work our agricul-turalists and pastoralists have accomplished hitherto in face of the very great odds they have had to meet. With comparatively little scientific training they have placed our wheat, wool and fruits in the highest estimation of the world; our sheep have been brought to such perfection that they're sought after not only by all the sister States but by South Africa.

Our agricultural machinery has been found good enough even for the Americans to copy; and our farming methods have been accepted by other States as the most up-to date and practical for Australian conditions. We have now reached a point when it behoves us to call science to our aid to a greater extent than hitherto has been done, otherwise we cannot hope to keep in the forefront.

In 1915 Peter Waite bought the Claremont Estate of 21 hectares and 45 hectares of the foothill part of the Netherby Estate, both of which adjoined Urrbrae, and transferred their ownership to the University of Adelaide. Before his death he set aside shares in Elder Smith and Co Ltd for the purpose of providing income to the University for the advancement of agricultural education.

Peter Waite was undoubtedly a generous man. He was a large contributor to public appeals in the later years of his life, for example to the Adelaide Children's Hospital and the Presbyterian Girls' School. Peter also paid for the bronze memorial to the members of the staff of Elder Smith and Co who served in World War I. He was one of South Australia's most significant public benefactors.

Peter and Matilda Waite died in 1922 in their 88th and 86th years respectively. In early 1923 the Urrbrae property was handed over to the University, which established the Waite Agricultural Research Institute on the site in 1924.

Three daughters, Elizabeth, Lily and Eva, survived their parents. With their brother James, they later made generous gifts to the University of Adelaide to support the work of the Waite Agricultural Research Institute.

RICHARD BOWYER SMITH 1837-1919

INVENTOR OF THE STUMP JUMP PLOUGH

RB Smith solved a major problem for farmers in the 'Mallee' and revolutionised wheat farming in South Australia and the world. Mallee, a eucalypt with a shallow root and multiple branches spreading out like an umbrella, covered much of the land suitable for wheat farming in South Australia. The Scrub Act of 1866 allowed leases of land with an option of purchase at one pound per acre after 21 years, but large areas could not be ploughed. This was a particular problem in the land bordering St Vincent Gulf and Yorke Peninsula, which was covered with mallee trees. This land near the coast allowed transport of the crop by ship to major markets and allowed farmers to compete successfully with the burgeoning wheat industry in California. However, the cost of clearing the land was about twice the cost of the land itself. After the trees were cut down, the roots sent up suckers which mixed in with the crops; they could be controlled by burning, but the roots and stumps remained, and greatly frustrated ploughing. Stump pullers were tried but either broke, were too heavy to use, or broke the stump and left the roots. Three skilled axemen cleared the land quicker than any machine.

In 1869 a farmer north of Gawler cut mallee to provide fuel for the nearby railway being built to Burra. To sow his wheat, he then dragged a log with spikes over the cleared ground and sowed grain in the furrows which resulted. His crop was successful and his name (Mullens) was immortalised in the term 'Mullenising'. This technique was widely applied, and he also found that the thin mallee trunks springing from the roots could be cleared by a heavy roller. After drying through the summer, the trunks and exposed roots were burned and after harvest the stubble was burned, which killed the new shoots. Mullenising worked for a while but the problem of roots and larger stumps remained.

RB Smith was a former agricultural machinery apprentice with a farm near Maitland on York Peninsula. In 1868 he built a three-furrow plough with each furrow on a hinge to let it rise when it hit an obstruction. A weight on each furrow caused it to re-enter the ground after passing the obstacle. It was eagerly adopted locally, and more widely at a later time when more furrows were added and the plough could be produced on an industrial scale. It appeared like 'a ship in a storm' but much of the land could be furrowed. It was just as useful on stony ground.

Following this success, the Scrub Lands Act was changed in 1877 to increase the amount of land which could be leased and reducing the moiety of land to be cleared annually to one-fortieth. Under the old Act, two-thirds of the land leased had been forfeited because clearing was too slow. In 1881 it was reported that after 600,000 acres had been selected under the new Act, less than five per cent of land had thus far been forfeited.

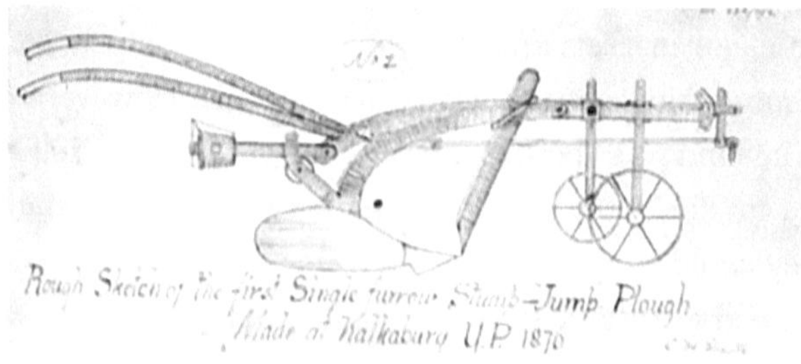

AFGHAN CAMEL DRIVERS 1859-1900

BULK TRANSPORT BEFORE RAILWAYS

Afghans are reported to have arrived in Australia in 1838, but the first camels (there were 24) came in 1860 with Afghan cameleers, to assist the ill-fated Burke and Wills expedition. Camels were the primary means of bulk transport in the country from 1850 to 1900, and were vital in building overland telegraph lines and railways.

In Kristin Wiedenbach's book *Mailman of the Birdsville Track – The story of Tom Kruse,* Tom remembers 'Ghan Town' on the northern side of the railway tracks, where the Afghans lived with the local Aborigines. Many came from Baluchistan on the border between Afghanistan and what is now Pakistan. They hardly recognised this European devised border and tended to move freely in the local hills; but whites used the term 'Afghan' in a derogatory way. They were brought to South Australia along with 122 camels from Karachi by pastoralists Samuel

Stuckey and Thomas Elder, to provide transport between their outlying pastoral runs after the Great Drought of 1864. They planted date palms and built mosques.

The Dervish Bejah Jakhrani Baloch (c.1862–1957), also known as Bejah Dervish, was an Australian camel driver who had a significant role in the exploration and development of inland Australia. When he was born in Baluchistan it was part of British India but since 1947 it has been part of Pakistan. He served with British forces at Kandahar and Karachi under Lord Roberts and attained the rank of sergeant. He arrived in Australia by sailing ship at the port of Fremantle in about 1890. In 1896 Bejah was engaged by Lawrence Wells to manage the camels used for transport on the ill-fated Calvert Scientific Exploring Expedition to the Great Sandy Desert of north-central Western Australia. In 1902 he settled in Marree, South Australia, where he bought land from which he operated his camel transport business.

On 15 December 1909 Baloch married Amelia Jane Shaw, a widow, and they had a son, Abdul Jubbar (Jack). In 1930 he retired from camel driving to grow date palms. Marree's original mosque was demolished in 1856; at that time Bejah was believed to be between 95 and 105 years old, and maintaining the mosque was 'a job for a younger man'. Another of the town's Afghan's elders, 86-year-old Syed Goolamdeen, had the mosque demolished and the woven prayer mat and silk-covered Koran were disposed of rather than have them ruined by neglect. Baloch was featured in the award-winning 1954 documentary film *The Back of Beyond*. On 6 May 1957 he died in the hospital at Port Augusta and was buried in the local cemetery. He is commemorated by a plaque on the Jubilee 150 Walkway in Adelaide, as someone who made a major contribution to the development of South Australia.

Trucks eventually took over the roles of the cameleers. There are stories of the old guard scattering nails on the road to thwart the new arrivals, but these are probably exaggerated. The Ghan Railway which now runs between Adelaide and Darwin (formerly the Afghan

Express) preserves the memory of the camel trade. The total number of Afghans who emigrated to Australia is estimated to be 3,000, with 2,000 arriving between 1870 and 1900. The oldest surviving mosque in Australia, built in 1888-1889, is in Adelaide. The next oldest (1905) is in Perth, Western Australia.

SIR HUBERT WILKINS 1888-1958

WAR HERO, ORNITHOLOGIST, EXPLORER AND PHOTOGRAPHER

Hubert Wilkins was born in Hallett, South Australia, and died in Framingham, Massachusetts, at the age of 70. He was known as a polar explorer, was a Knight Bachelor with Military Cross and Bar, and he was also an ornithologist, pilot, soldier, geographer and photographer. After his 1928 flight across the Arctic he was given a tickertape parade in New York.

Hubert was the last of 13 children in a family of pioneer settlers and sheep farmers. He was born at Mount Bryan, South Australia, 177 kilometres north of Adelaide by road. The original homestead has been restored by generous donation. He was educated at Mount Bryan East and the Adelaide School of Mines. As a teenager, he moved to Adelaide where he found work with a travelling cinema, went to Sydney as a cinematographer, and then to England where he became a pioneering aerial photographer whilst working for Gaumont Studios.

His photographic skill earned him a place on various Arctic expeditions, including the controversial 1913 Canadian Arctic Expedition led by Vilhjalmur Stefansson.

In 1917, Wilkins returned to his native Australia and joined the Australian Flying Corps in the rank of Second Lieutenant. Wilkins later transferred to the general list and in 1918 was appointed as an official war photographer. In June 1918, Wilkins was awarded the Military Cross for his efforts to rescue wounded soldiers during the Third Battle of Ypres. He remains the only Australian official photographer from any war to have received a combat medal.

The following month, Wilkins was promoted to Captain and became the officer commanding No.3 (Photographic) Sub-section of the Australian War Records Unit. Unfortunately, due to his modest nature, many iconic WWI photographs have been attributed to (or even claimed by) the self-promoting Frank Hurley. For example, the famous photograph of dazed Australian soldiers walking the duckboards through Chateau Wood on 29 October 1917 has always been credited to Hurley, but Hurley's diary reveals that he was nowhere near Chateau Wood on that day.

Wilkins' work frequently led him into the thick of the fighting, and during the Battle of the Hindenburg Line he assumed command of a group of American soldiers who had lost their officers in an earlier attack, directing them until support arrived. Wilkins was subsequently awarded a bar to his Military Cross in the 1919 Birthday Honours. When Sir John Monash was asked by the visiting American journalist Lowell Thomas (who had written *Lawrence of Arabia*, making him an international hero) if Australia had a similar hero, Monash replied:

Yes, there was one. He was a highly accomplished and absolutely fearless combat photographer. What happened to him is a story of epic proportions. Wounded many times ... he always came through. At times he brought in the wounded, at other times he supplied vital intelligence of enemy activity he observed. At one point he even rallied troops as a combat officer ... His record was unique.

After the war, Wilkins served in 1921–1922 as an ornithologist aboard the *Quest*, on the Shackleton-Rowett Expedition to the Southern Ocean and adjacent islands.

In 1923 Wilkins began a two-year study for the British Museum of the bird life of Northern Australia. This ornithology project occupied his life until 1925. His work was greatly acclaimed by the British Museum but derided by Australian authorities because of the sympathetic treatment afforded the Aborigines and criticisms of the ongoing environmental damage in the country.

In March 1927, Wilkins and pilot Carl Ben Eielson explored the drift ice north of Alaska, touching down upon it in Eielson's aeroplane in the first land-plane descent onto drift ice. Soundings taken at the landing site indicated a water depth of 16,000 feet, and Wilkins hypothesised from the experience that future Arctic expeditions would take advantage of the wide expanses of open ice to use aircraft in exploration.

Wilkins was the first recipient of the Samuel Finley Breese Morse Medal, which was awarded to him by the American Geographical Society in 1928. He was also awarded the Royal Geographical Society's Patron's Gold Medal in the same year.

On 15 April 1928, only a year after Charles Lindbergh's flight across the Atlantic, Wilkins and Eielson made a trans-Arctic crossing from Point Barrow, Alaska, to Spitsbergen, arriving about 20 hours later on 16 April, touching along the way at Grant Land on Ellesmere Island. For this feat and his prior work Wilkins was knighted, and during the ensuing celebration in New York he met Australian actress, Suzanne Bennett, whom he later married. Now financed by William Randolph Hearst, Wilkins continued his polar explorations, flying over Antarctica in the *San Francisco*. He named Hearst Land after his sponsor, and Hearst thanked Wilkins by giving him and his bride a flight aboard *Graf Zeppelin*.

In 1930 Wilkins and his wife, Suzanne, were vacationing with a wealthy friend and colleague Lincoln Ellsworth. During this outing Wilkins and Ellsworth hammered out plans for a trans-Arctic expedition involving a submarine. Wilkins said the expedition was meant to conduct a 'comprehensive meteorology study' and collect 'data of academic and economic interest'. He also anticipated Arctic weather stations and the potential to forecast Arctic weather 'several years in advance'. Wilkins believed a submarine could take a fully equipped laboratory into the Arctic. Ellsworth contributed $70,000, plus a $20,000 loan. Hearst purchased exclusive rights to the story for $61,000. The Woods Hole Oceanographic Institute contributed a further $35,000. Finally, Wilkins himself used $25,000 of his own money. Since Wilkins was not a US citizen, he was unable to purchase the 1918 submarine scheduled to be decommissioned. However, he was permitted to lease the vessel for a period of five years at a cost of one dollar annually from Lake and Danenhower, Inc.

The submarine was the disarmed O-12, and was commanded by Sloan Danenhower (former commanding officer of C-4). Wilkins renamed her *Nautilus*, after Jules Verne's vessel in *20,000 Leagues Under the Sea*. The submarine was outfitted with a custom-designed drill that would allow her to bore through ice pack overhead for ventilation. The crew of eighteen men was chosen with great care. Among their ranks were US Naval Academy graduates as well as navy veterans of World War I. Wilkins described the planned expedition in his 1931 book *Under the North Pole*, which Wonder Stories praised as '[as] exciting as it is epochal'.

The expedition suffered losses before they even left New York Harbour. Willard Grimmer the quartermaster was knocked overboard and drowned. Wilkins was undaunted and drove on with preparations for a series of test cruises and dives before they were to undertake their trans-Atlantic voyage. Wilkins and his crew made their way up the Hudson River to Yonkers, eventually reaching New London, Connecticut, where additional modifications and test dives were performed. Satisfied with the performance of both the machinery and the crew, Wilkins and his men left the relative safety of coastal waterways for the uncertainty of the North Atlantic on 4 June 1931. Soon after the commencement of the expedition the starboard engine broke down, and soon after that the port engine followed suit. On 14 June

1931, without a means of propulsion, Wilkins was forced to send out an SOS and was rescued later that day by the *USS Wyoming*. The *Nautilus* was towed to Ireland on 22 June 1931, and later was taken to England for repairs.

On 28 June the *Nautilus* was up and running and on her way to Norway to pick up the scientific contingent of their crew. By 23 August they had left Norway and were only 600 miles from the North Pole. It was at this time that Wilkins uncovered another setback: his submarine was missing its diving planes. Without them, he would be unable to control the *Nautilus* while submerged. Wilkins secretly felt that his mission was deliberately sabotaged by a crew member. He was determined to do what he could without the diving planes. For the most part, Wilkins was thwarted from discovery under the ice floes. However, the crew was able to take core samples of the ice, as well as testing of the salinity of the water, and of gravity near the pole.

The *Nautilus* expedition had suffered one setback after another, but they continued on bravely. However, even Wilkins had to acknowledge when his adventure into the Arctic was becoming too foolhardy. Wilkins received a wireless plea from one of his financiers, Hearst, which said, 'I most urgently beg of you to return promptly to safety and to defer any further adventure to a more favourable time, and with a better boat.' Wilkins ended the first expedition to the poles in a submarine and headed for England, but he was forced to take refuge in the port of Bergen, Norway, because of a fierce storm that they encountered en route. The *Nautilus* suffered serious damage that made further use of the vessel unfeasible. Wilkins received permission from the United States Navy to sink the vessel offshore in a Norwegian fjord on 20 November 1931. Despite the failure to meet his intended objective, he was able to prove that submarines were capable of operating beneath the polar ice cap, thereby paving the way for future successful missions.

Wilkins became a student of *The Urantia Book* and supporter of the Urantia movement after joining the secretive Forum group in Chicago in 1942. After the book's publication in 1955, he 'carried the massive work on his long travels, even to the Antarctic' and told associates that it was his religion. On 16 March 1958, Wilkins appeared as a guest on the TV panel show *What's My Line?* He died in Framingham, Massachusetts, on 30 November 1958 and the US Navy took his ashes to the North Pole aboard the submarine *USS Skate* on 17 March 1959. The Navy confirmed on 27 March that: 'In a solemn memorial ceremony conducted by *Skate* shortly after surfacing, the ashes of Sir Hubert Wilkins were scattered at the North Pole in accordance with his last wishes.'

The Wilkins Sound, Wilkins Coast and the Wilkins Ice Shelf in Antarctica are named after him, as are the airport at Jamestown, South Australia, and a road at Adelaide Airport. The majority of Wilkins' papers and effects are archived at The Ohio State University Byrd Polar Research Center. A species of Australian skink, *Lerista wilkinsi*, is named after him.

LAWRENCE BRAGG 1890-1971

WINNER OF NOBEL PRIZE FOR INVENTION OF X-RAY CRYSTALLOGRAPHY

Sir William Lawrence Bragg CH OBE MC FRS was an Australian-born British physicist and x-ray crystallographer. In 1912 he discovered Bragg's Law which is basic for the determination of crystal structure. With his father, William Henry Bragg, he was joint winner of the Nobel Prize in Physics in 1915, 'for their services in the analysis of crystal structure by means of X-ray', an important step in the development of X-ray crystallography.

Bragg was knighted in 1941. As of 2018, he was the youngest ever Nobel laureate in physics, having received the award at the age of 25 years. Bragg was the Director of the Cavendish Laboratory, Cambridge, when the discovery of the structure of DNA was reported by James D Watson and Francis Crick in February 1953. The discovery relied upon X-ray crystallography to define the double helix and this work was done by Rosalind Franklin, who is largely unrecognised. She did not receive the Nobel Prize for Medicine (as Watson and Crick did) because she had died and the Prize is never awarded posthumously.

Bragg was born in Adelaide, South Australia. He showed an early interest in science and mathematics. His father, William Henry Bragg, was Elder Professor of Mathematics and Physics at the University of Adelaide. Shortly after starting school, William Lawrence Bragg fell from his tricycle and broke his arm. His father had read about Röntgen's experiments in Europe and was performing his own experiments, so he used the newly discovered X-rays and his experimental equipment to examine the broken arm. This is the first recorded surgical use of X-rays in Australia.

Bragg began his studies in 1905 at St Peter's College, Adelaide, and went to the University of Adelaide at the age of 16 to study mathematics, chemistry and physics, graduating in 1908. In the same year his father accepted the Cavendish Chair of Physics at the University of Leeds, and brought the family to England. Lawrence entered Trinity College, Cambridge, in the autumn of 1909 and received a major scholarship in mathematics, despite taking the exam while in bed with pneumonia. After initially excelling in mathematics, he transferred to the physics course in the later years of his studies, and graduated with First Class Honours in 1911. In 1914 Bragg was elected to a Fellowship at Trinity College after his successful submission and defence of a thesis.

Among Bragg's other interests was shell collecting; his personal collection amounted to specimens from some 500 species, all personally collected from South Australia. He discovered a new species of cuttlefish, which Joseph Verco named *Sepia braggi* for him.

The composition of X-rays was unknown. Bragg's father argued that X-rays were streams of particles; others argued that they were waves. Max von Laue directed an X-ray beam at a crystal in front of a photographic plate, and alongside the spot where the beam struck there were additional spots from deflected rays; this showed that X-rays are waves. In 1912, as a first-year research student at Cambridge, Lawrence Bragg, while strolling by the river, had the insight that crystals made from parallel sheets of atoms would not diffract X-ray beams that struck their surface at most angles because X-rays deflected by collisions with atoms would be out of phase, cancelling one another out. However, when the X-ray beam struck at an angle at which the distances it passed between atomic sheets in the crystal equalled the X-ray's wavelength, then those deflected would be in phase and produce a spot on a nearby film. From this insight he wrote the simple *Bragg equation* that relates the wavelength of the X-ray and the distance between atomic sheets in a simple crystal to the angles at which an impinging X-ray beam would be reflected.

Bragg's father built an apparatus in which a crystal could be rotated to precise angles while measuring the energy of reflections. This enabled father and son to measure the distances between the atomic sheets in a number of simple crystals. They calculated the spacing of the atoms from the weight of the crystal and Avogadro's constant, which enabled them to measure the wavelengths of the X-rays produced by different metallic targets in the X-ray tubes. WH Bragg reported their results at meetings and in a paper, giving credit to 'his son' (unnamed) for the equation, but not as a co-author, which gave his son 'some heartaches' which he never overcame.

Lawrence was commissioned early in the First World War in the Royal Horse Artillery, as a second lieutenant of the Leicestershire battery. In 1915 he was seconded to the Royal Engineers to develop a method to localise enemy artillery from the boom of their firing. On 2 September 1915 his brother was killed during the Gallipoli Campaign. Shortly afterwards, when he was 25 years old, he and his father were awarded the Nobel Prize in Physics. The problem with sound ranging was that the heavy guns boomed at too low a frequency to be detected by a microphone. After months of frustrating failure, he and his group devised a hot wire air wave detector that solved the problem. In this work he was aided by Charles Galton Darwin, William Sansome Tucker, Harold Roper Robinson and Henry Harold Hemming. British sound ranging was very effective; there was a unit in every British Army and their system was adopted by the Americans when they entered the war. For his work during the war, Lawrence Bragg was awarded the Military

Cross and appointed Officer of the Order of the British Empire. He was also Mentioned in Despatches on 16 June 1916, 4 January 1917 and 7 July 1919.

When demobilised he returned to crystallography at Cambridge. He and his father had agreed that the father would study organic crystals, and the son would investigate inorganic compounds. In 1919 when Ernest Rutherford, a long-time family friend, moved to Cambridge, Lawrence Bragg replaced him as Langworthy Professor of Physics at the Victoria University of Manchester. He recruited an excellent faculty, including former sound rangers, but he believed that his knowledge of physics was weak and he had no classroom experience. The students, many veterans, were critical and rowdy. He was deeply shaken but with family support he pulled himself together and prevailed. He and RW James measured the absolute energy of reflected X-rays, which validated a formula derived by CG Darwin before the war. Now they could determine the number of electrons in the reflecting targets, and they were able to decipher the structures of more complicated crystals like silicates. It was still difficult, requiring repeated guessing and retrying. In the late 1920s they eased the analysis by using Fourier transforms on the data.

In 1930 he became deeply disturbed while weighing a job offer from Imperial College, London. His family rallied around and he recovered his balance while they spent 1931 in Munich, where he did research.

He became Director of the National Physical Laboratory (NPL) in Teddington in 1937, bringing some co-workers along. However, administration and committees took much of his time away from the workbench.

Rutherford died and the search committee named Lawrence Bragg as next in the line of the Cavendish Professors who direct the Cavendish Laboratory. The Laboratory had an eminent history in atomic physics and some members were wary of a crystallographer, which Bragg surmounted by even-handed administration. He worked on improving the interpretation of diffraction patterns. In the small crystallography group was a refugee research student without a mentor, Max Perutz.

He showed Bragg X-ray diffraction data from haemoglobin, which suggested that the structure of giant biological molecules might be deciphered. Bragg appointed Perutz as his research assistant and within a few months obtained additional support with a grant from the Rockefeller Foundation. The work was suspended during the Second World War when Perutz was interned as an enemy alien and then worked in military research.

During the war the Cavendish offered a shortened graduate course which emphasised the electronics needed for radar. Bragg worked on the structure of metals and consulted on sonar and sound ranging. He became Sir Lawrence in 1941. His father died in 1942. During that year Bragg served for six months as Scientific Liaison Officer to Canada, and organised periodic conferences on X-ray analysis, which was widely used in military research.

After the war he led in the formation of the International Union of Crystallography and was elected its first President. He reorganised the Cavendish into units to reflect his conviction that 'the ideal research unit is one of six to twelve scientists and a few assistants, helped by one or more first-class instrument mechanics and a workshop in which the general run of apparatus can be constructed'. Senior members of staff now had offices, telephones and secretarial support. The scope of the department was enlarged with a new unit on radio astronomy.

Bragg's own work focused on the structure of metals, using both X-rays and the electron microscope. In 1947 he persuaded the Medical Research Council to support what he described as the 'gallant attempt' to determine protein structure as the Laboratory of Molecular Biology (MRC), initially consisting of Perutz, John Kendrew and two assistants. Bragg worked with them, and by 1960 they had resolved the structure of myoglobin to the atomic level. After this he was less involved. The first monumental triumph of the MRC was decoding the structure of DNA by James Watson and Francis Crick.

Bragg announced the discovery at a Solvay conference on proteins in Belgium on 8 April 1953, but it went unreported by the press. He then gave a talk at Guy's Hospital Medical School in London on

Thursday 14 May 1953, which resulted in an article by Ritchie Calder in the *News Chronicle* of London on Friday 15 May 1953, entitled *Why You Are You. Nearer Secret of Life*. Bragg nominated Crick, Watson and Maurice Wilkins for the 1962 Nobel Prize in Physiology or Medicine; Wilkins' share recognised the contribution of X-ray crystallographers at King's College London. Among them was Rosalind Franklin, whose 'photograph 51' showed that DNA was a double helix, not the triple helix that Linus Pauling had proposed. Franklin died before the prize (which only goes to living people) was awarded.

In 1953 the Braggs moved into the elegant flat for the Resident Professor in the Royal Institution in London, the position his father had occupied when he died. In 1931 and 1934 Lawrence had delivered the Royal Institution Christmas Lecture and since 1938 he had been Professor of Natural Philosophy in the Institution, delivering an annual lecture. His father's successors had weakened the Institution, so Lawrence had to rebuild. He bolstered finances by enlisting corporate sponsors; the traditional Friday Evening Discourses were followed by a dinner party for the speaker and carefully selected possible patrons, and there were more than one hundred and twenty of them each year. Two of these Discourses in 1965 gave him particular pleasure. On 7 May, Lady Bragg, who had been a member of the Royal Commission on Marriage and Divorce (1951-55) and was Chairman of the National Marriage Guidance Council, lectured on *Changing patterns in marriage and divorce*; and on 15 November, Bragg listened with evident pride to the Discourse on 'Oscillations and noise in jet engines' given by his engineer son Stephen, who was then Chief Scientist at Rolls Royce Ltd and later became Vice-Chancellor of Brunel University. He also introduced a new programme of highly regarded Schools' Lectures, enlivened by the elaborate demonstrations that were a hallmark of the Institution. He gave three of these lectures on 'electricity'.

He continued research in the Institution by recruiting a small group to work the Davy-Faraday Laboratory in the basement and in the adjoining house, supported by grants he obtained. A visitor to the laboratory succeeded in inserting heavy metals into the enzyme lysozyme;

the structure of its crystal was solved in 1965 at the Royal Institution by DC Phillips and his co-workers, with the computations on the 9,040 reflections performed on the digital computer at the University of London, which greatly facilitated the work. Two of the illustrations of the positioning of amino acids in the chain were drawn by Bragg. Unlike myoglobin, in which nearly 80 percent of the amino-acid residues are in the alpha-helix conformation, in lysozyme the alpha-helix content is only about 40 percent of the amino-acid residues found in four main stretches. Other stretches are of the 3_{10} helix, a conformation that they had proposed earlier. In this conformation, every third peptide is hydrogen-bonded back to the first peptide, thus forming a ring containing ten atoms. They had the complete structure of an enzyme in time for Bragg's seventy-fifth birthday. He became Professor Emeritus in 1966.

X-ray analysis of protein structure flourished in subsequent years, determining the structures of scores of proteins in laboratories around the world. Twenty-eight Nobel Prizes have been awarded for work using X-ray analysis. The disadvantage of the method is that it must be done on crystals, which precludes seeing changes in shape when enzymes bind substrates and the like. This problem was solved by the development of another line Bragg had initiated, using modified electron microscopes to image single frozen molecules: cryo-electron microscopy.

In his long association with the Royal Institution Lawrence Bragg was:

    Professor of Natural Philosophy, 1938–1953

    Fullerian Professor of Chemistry, 1954–1966

    Superintendent of the House, 1954–1966

    Director of the Davy-Faraday Research Laboratory, 1954–1966

    Director of the Royal Institution, 1965–1966

    Emeritus Professor, 1966–1971.

In 1921 he married Alice Hopkinson (1899–1989), a cousin of a friend who had been killed in the war. They had four children, Stephen

Lawrence (1923–2014), David William (1926–2005), Margaret Alice, born 1931 (who married Mark Heath), and Patience Mary, born 1935. Alice was on the staff at Withington Girls' School until Bragg was appointed director of the NPL in 1937. She was active in a number of public bodies and was elected Mayor of Cambridge.

Bragg's hobbies included drawing — family letters were illustrated with lively sketches — painting, literature and a lifelong interest in gardening. When he moved to London, he missed having a garden and worked as a part-time gardener, unrecognised by his employer, until a guest at the house expressed surprise at seeing him there. He died at a hospital near his home at Waldringfield, Ipswich, Suffolk. He was buried in Trinity College, Cambridge; his son David is buried in the Parish of the Ascension Burial Ground in Cambridge, where Bragg's friend Rudolph Cecil Hopkinson, who had he survived would have been his brother-in-law, is also buried.

Bragg was elected a Fellow of the Royal Society (FRS) in 1921 – described as 'a qualification that makes other ones irrelevant'. He was knighted by King George VI in the 1941 New Year Honours, and received both the Copley Medal and the Royal Medal of the Royal Society. In his book on Bragg, *Light is a Messenger*, Graeme Hunter argued that he was more a crystallographer than a physicist, but Bragg's lifelong activity showed otherwise - he was more of a physicist than anything else. Thus, from 1939 to 1943, he served as President of the Institute of Physics, London. In the 1967 New Year Honours he was appointed Companion of Honour by Queen Elizabeth II.

Since 1992, the Australian Institute of Physics has awarded the Bragg Gold Medal for Excellence in Physics to commemorate Lawrence Bragg (in front on the medal) and his father, William Bragg, for the best PhD thesis by a student at an Australian university.

Lawrence Bragg's awards include: Nobel Prize (1915), Matteucci Medal (1915), Hughes Medal (1931), Royal Medal (1946), Guthrie Lecture (1952) and Copley Medal (1966).

RA FISHER 1890-1962

CREATOR OF MODERN STATISTICS

Sir Ronald Aylmer Fisher FRS, who published as RA Fisher, is buried in St Peters Cathedral in Adelaide. He was a British statistician and geneticist. For his work in statistics, he has been described as 'a genius who almost single-handedly created the foundations for modern statistical science' and 'the single most important figure in 20th century statistics'. In genetics, his work used mathematics to combine Mendelian genetics and natural selection; this contributed to the revival of Darwinism in the early 20th century revision of the theory of evolution known as the modern synthesis. Fisher also did experimental agricultural research, which has saved millions from starvation.

Fisher was born in East Finchley in London, England, into a middle-class family; his father, George, was a successful partner in Robinson and Fisher, auctioneers and fine art dealers. Ronald was one of twins, but the other was still-born; and he grew up the youngest with three sisters and one brother. From 1896 until 1904 they lived at

Inverforth House in London, where English Heritage installed a blue plaque in 2002; they later moved to Streatham. His mother, Kate, died from acute peritonitis when he was 14, and his father lost his business 18 months later.

Lifelong poor eyesight caused Fisher's rejection by the British Army for World War I, but it also contributed to the development of his ability to visualise problems in geometrical terms rather than in writing mathematical solutions, or proofs. He entered Harrow School aged 14 and won the school's Neeld Medal in Mathematics. In 1909, he won a scholarship to study Mathematics at Gonville and Caius College, Cambridge. In 1912, he gained a First in Astronomy. In 1915 he published a paper titled *The evolution of sexual preference on sexual selection and mate choice.*

From 1913-1919, Fisher worked for six years as a statistician in the City of London and taught physics and maths at a sequence of public schools, at the Thames Nautical Training College, and at Bradfield College. There he settled with his new bride, Eileen Guinness, with whom he had two sons and six daughters.

In 1918 he published *The Correlation Between Relatives on the Supposition of Mendelian Inheritance*, in which he introduced the term 'variance' and proposed its formal analysis. He put forward a genetics conceptual model showing that continuous variation amongst phenotypic traits measured by biostatisticians could be produced by the combined action of many discrete genes and thus be the result of Mendelian inheritance. This was the first step towards establishing population genetics and quantitative genetics, which demonstrated that natural selection could change allele frequencies in a population, resulting in reconciling its discontinuous nature with gradual evolution. Joan Box, Fisher's daughter and biographer, says that Fisher had resolved this problem already in 1911. In 1919, he began working at the Rothamsted Experimental Station. During his 14 years there he analysed its immense data from crop experiments since the 1840s, the 'Classical Field Experiments', and developed the analysis of variance (ANOVA). In 1928, Joseph Oscar Irwin began a three-year stint at Rothamsted and became one of the first people to master Fisher's innovations.

Fisher's 1924 article *On a distribution yielding the error functions of several well known statistics* presented Pearson's chi-squared test and William Gosset's Student's t-distribution in the same framework as the Gaussian distribution; this is where he developed Fisher's z-distribution, a new statistical method, commonly used decades later as the F distribution. He pioneered the principles of the design of experiments, the statistics of small samples and the analysis of real data.

In 1925 he published *Statistical Methods for Research Workers*, one of the 20th century's most influential books on statistical methods. Fisher's method is a technique for data fusion or 'meta-analysis' (analysis of analyses). This book also popularised the p-value, and it plays a central role in this approach. Fisher proposes the level $p=0.05$, or a 1 in 20 chance of being exceeded by chance, as a limit for statistical significance, and applies this to a normal distribution (as a two-tailed test), thus yielding the rule of two standard deviations (on a normal distribution) for statistical significance. The 1.96, the approximate value of the 97.5 percentile point of the normal distribution used in probability and statistics, also originated in this book: *The value for which P=.05, or 1 in 20, is 1.96 or nearly 2; it is convenient to take this point as a limit in judging whether a deviation is to be considered significant or not.* In Table 1 of the work, he gave the more precise value 1.959964.

In 1928, Fisher was the first to use diffusion equations to attempt to calculate the distribution of allele frequencies and the estimation of genetic linkage by maximum likelihood methods among populations. In 1930, *The Genetical Theory of Natural Selection* was first published by Clarendon Press and is dedicated to Leonard Darwin. A core work of the neo-Darwinian modern evolutionary synthesis, it helped define population genetics, which Fisher founded alongside Sewall Wright and JBS Haldane, and revived Darwin's neglected idea of sexual selection. One of Fisher´s favourite aphorisms was: 'Natural selection is a mechanism for generating an exceedingly high degree of improbability'. Richard Dawkins later wrote a book titled *Climbing Mount Improbable*.

Not well understood even now, is the non-blending nature of heredity, an idea starting with Mendel's discovery in 1865. In his book *The Greatest Show on Earth*, Richard Dawkins says:

the theory culminated in the work of the great geneticist and statistician Ronald Fisher and, again largely independently, his co-founders of population genetics, JBS Haldane and Sewall Wright.

Fisher´s fame grew and he began to travel and lecture widely. In 1931, he spent six weeks at the Statistical Laboratory at Iowa State College, where he gave three lectures per week, and met many American statisticians, including George W Snedecor. He returned there again in 1936.

In 1933, Fisher became the Head of the Department of Eugenics at University College London. In 1935, he published *The Design of Experiments*, which was 'also fundamental, [and promoted] statistical technique and application... The mathematical justification of the methods was not stressed and proofs were often barely sketched or omitted altogether .... [This] led H.B. Mann to fill the gaps with a rigorous mathematical treatment'. In this book Fisher also outlined the *Lady tasting tea*, now a famous design of a statistical randomised experiment which uses Fisher's Exact Test and is the original exposition of Fisher's notion of a null hypothesis. The same year he also published a paper on fiducial inference and applied it to the Behrens–Fisher problem, the solution to which, proposed first by Walter Behrens and a few years later by Fisher, is the Behrens–Fisher distribution.

In 1936 he introduced the Iris flower data set as an example of discriminant analysis. In his 1937 paper *The wave of advance of advantageous genes*, he proposed Fisher's equation in the context of population dynamics to describe the spatial spread of an advantageous allele, and explored its travelling wave solutions. Out of this also came the Fisher-Kolmogorov equation. In 1937, he visited the Indian Statistical Institute in Calcutta, and its one part-time employee, PC Mahalanobis, often returning to encourage its development. He was the guest of honour at the Institute's 25th anniversary in 1957, when it had 2000 employees.

In 1938, Fisher and Frank Yates described the Fisher-Yates shuffle in their book *Statistical tables for biological, agricultural and medical research*. Their description of the algorithm used pencil and paper; a table of random numbers provided the randomness.

In 1943, along with AS Corbet and CB Williams he published a paper on relative species abundance where he developed the logseries to fit two different abundance data sets. In the same year he took the Balfour Chair of Genetics at the University of Cambridge, where the Italian researcher Luigi Luca Cavalli-Sforza was recruited in 1948, establishing a one-man unit of bacterial genetics. In 1936, Fisher used a Pearson's chi-squared test to analyse Mendel's data and concluded that Mendel's results with the predicted ratios were far too perfect, suggesting that adjustments (intentional or unconscious) had been made to the data to make the observations fit the hypothesis. Later authors have claimed Fisher's analysis was flawed, proposing various statistical and botanical explanations for Mendel's numbers. In 1947, Fisher co-founded the journal *Heredity* with Cyril Darlington, and in 1949 he published *The Theory of Inbreeding*.

In 1950 he published *Gene Frequencies in a Cline Determined by Selection and Diffusion* on the wave of advance of advantageous genes and on clines of gene frequency; this was notable as the first application of a computer, the EDSAC, to biology. He developed computational algorithms for analysing data from his balanced experimental designs, with various editions and translations, becoming a standard reference work for scientists in many disciplines. In ecological genetics he and EB Ford showed how the force of natural selection was much stronger than had been assumed, with many ecogenetic situations (such as polymorphism) being maintained by the force of selection. During this time he also worked on mouse chromosome mapping, breeding the mice in laboratories in his own house.

Fisher publicly spoke out against the 1950 study showing that smoking tobacco causes lung cancer, arguing that correlation does not imply causation. To quote his biographers Yates and Mather:

It has been suggested that the fact that Fisher was employed as consultant by the tobacco firms in this controversy casts doubt on the value of his arguments. This is to misjudge the man. He was not above accepting financial reward for his labours, but the reason for his interest was undoubtedly his dislike and mistrust of puritanical tendencies of all kinds; and perhaps also the personal solace he had always found in tobacco.

He has been reported as smoking in a front seat at meetings of the (now defunct) Medical Sciences Club in Adelaide and saying, 'it hasn't been proved that smoking causes lung cancer'.

Fisher held strong views on race. Throughout his life, he was a prominent supporter of eugenics, an interest which led to his work on statistics and genetics. Notably, he was a dissenting voice in UNESCO's statement *The Race Question,* insisting on racial differences.

In the winter of 1954–1955, Fisher met Debabrata Basu, the Indian statistician who wrote in 1988:

With his reference set argument, Sir Ronald was trying to find a viable medium between the two poles of Statistics – Berkeley and Bayes. My efforts to understand this Fisher compromise led me to the likelihood principle.

In 1957, Fisher emigrated to South Australia, where he spent time as a senior Research Fellow at the Australian Commonwealth Scientific and Industrial Research Organisation (CSIRO) in Adelaide. He died there in 1962, and his remains were interred within St Peter's Cathedral.

ROSS SMITH 1892–1922

WAR HERO AND PIONEER AVIATOR

Ross Macpherson Smith, airman, was born in Adelaide. He was the son of Scottish-born Andrew Bell Smith, station manager, and his wife Jessie, née Macpherson, who was born in Western Australia. In 1919 Ross and his brother Keith, together with mechanics WH Shiers and JM Bennett, became the first pilots to fly from Britain to Australia in 30 days. The historic Vickers Vimy in which they flew is displayed at Adelaide Airport. It is one of the world's most significant aviation relics and will have a new showcase built for it at a price of $6 million. South Australia's chief entrepreneur, Jim Whalley, Chair of defence company Nova Systems, said that it's 'a real example of the sort of entrepreneurship on which SA was founded'.

Both Ross and his brother Keith were educated at Queen's School, Adelaide as boarders, where the principal claimed they were steady but would not 'set the world on fire'; and for two years at Warriston School, Moffat, Scotland, their father's birthplace.

On his return to Australia, Ross joined the Australian Mounted Cadets and was selected in 1910 to tour Britain and the United States of America as a South Australian representative. He then joined the 10th Australian Regiment, the Adelaide Rifles. Before the outbreak of war in 1914, Ross was employed as a warehouseman in Adelaide for GP Harris Scarfe and Co. In August 1914 he enlisted as a Private in the 3rd Light Horse Regiment, Australian Imperial Forces (AIF), and on 1 October was promoted to Sergeant. He embarked for Egypt on 22 October and landed on Gallipoli on 13 May 1915. On 11 August he attained the rank of Regimental Sergeant Major and was commissioned Second Lieutenant on 5 September. Invalided to England in October, he was promoted to Lieutenant on 1 March 1916, and three weeks later embarked for Egypt to rejoin his old regiment. With the 1st Light Horse Brigade, 1st Machine-Gun Squadron, his principal action occurred during the battle of Romani on 4 August 1916. In July 1917 he responded to a call for volunteers to join the Australian Flying Corps, and the transfer took effect on 4 August.

Ross and Keith had different early careers, but both brothers entered aviation within weeks of each other. On the outbreak of war, Keith, employed by Elder Smith and Co in Adelaide, was rejected for service with the AIF on medical grounds. He underwent medical treatment and paid his own passage to England to enlist in the Royal Flying Corps. He was accepted into the Officer Cadet Wing in July 1917 and posted in November to No.58 Squadron, a newly formed bomber unit which left for France in January 1918. However, Keith did not see active service, apparently due to his varicose veins. On 24 February 1918 he was posted to No.5 Squadron, a home-defence formation, as a gunnery instructor. On 1 April he was promoted to Lieutenant and spent the rest of the war in Britain with training establishments. He was placed on the unemployed list, RAF, on 5 November 1919.

In contrast, Ross's air war was more brilliant. Qualifying as an observer in December 1916, and later as a pilot, he served mainly with No.1 Squadron, Australian Flying Corps (No.67 Squadron RFC), a general purpose squadron flying a variety of aircraft in defence of the Suez Canal zone. In January 1918 it was re-equipped with the Bristol Fighter and designated a fighter squadron. The squadron was an important element of General (Lord) Allenby's 1918 offensive and took part in the overwhelming air attacks on the Turkish armies in the Wadi Fara. By the end of the war Ross had twice been decorated with the Military Cross and three times with the Distinguished Flying Cross. He reportedly downed ten enemy aircraft. Later he added the Air Force Cross for non-operational flying. The first Military Cross was awarded while Ross, still an observer, landed in the face of the enemy to rescue a fellow officer who had been brought down. Bombing, photography and air-to-air combats brought the other operational awards.

By the end of the war Ross had acquired considerable experience flying the twin-engined Handley Page 0/400 bomber which had been attached to the squadron. He had flown it not only on bombing operations in Palestine but also on long photographic flights. He was consequently selected to co-pilot the aircraft in a pioneer flight from Cairo to Calcutta, leaving Cairo on 29 November 1918 and arriving in Calcutta on 10 December. A tentative attempt was made from Calcutta to survey an aerial route through to Australia. This was abandoned at Timor. Nevertheless, the experience gained was of great benefit in the successful attempt later undertaken with his brother to fly from England to Australia within thirty days. The prize of £10,000 was offered by the Australian Government for the first aviator to do so.

The attempt began from Hounslow, England, on 12 November 1919, in a Vickers Vimy (a type similiar to the 0/400 bomber) supplied by the manufacturer, and with Keith as assistant pilot and navigator and accompanied by two mechanics. Flying conditions were very poor and extremely hazardous until they reached Basra on 22 November. From Basra to Delhi, a distance of 1600 miles (2575 km), they spent 25½ hours in the air out of 54. A poor landing-area at Singora and torrential rain almost brought disaster on 3 December. Disaster again almost came at Surabaya, where the aircraft was bogged and had to take off from an improvised airstrip made of bamboo mats. However, by 9 December they were at Timor, only 350 miles (563 km) from Darwin. The crossing was made next day and at 3.50 pm on 10 December they landed in Darwin. The distance covered in this epic flight was 18,250 km (11,340 miles). It took just under 28 days with an actual flying time of 135 hours at an average speed of 137 kph (85 mph). Both Ross and Keith were immediately knighted; Sergeants WH Shiers and JM Bennett, the mechanics, were commissioned and awarded Bars to their Air Force Medals, and the £10,000 prize money was divided into four equal shares.

The next proposal, to fly round the world in a Vickers Viking amphibian, ended in disaster. Both brothers travelled to England to prepare for the trip and on 13 April 1922, while Ross and his long-serving crew member Bennett were test-flying the aircraft at Weybridge near London, it spun into the ground from 1000 feet (305 m), killing both. Keith, who arrived late for the test flight, witnessed the accident. Ross had not flown at all for many months and had never flown this type of aircraft. The investigating committee concluded that the accident had been the result of pilot error. The flight was abandoned. The bodies of Sir Ross Smith and Lieutenant Bennett were brought home to Australia and after a state funeral Smith was buried in Adelaide on 15 June.

Sir Keith Smith was appointed Australian agent for Vickers and retained the connexion with this British company until his death. Between the wars, however, Vickers took little interest in the small Australian market and despite Smith's efforts, there was no sale of aircraft until the arrival of the Viscount in 1954. One promising venture strongly supported by Ross Smith in the early 1920s was to employ Vickers-built airships on Imperial air routes. A British airship had successfully crossed the Atlantic in July 1919, but projects failed to materialise. The British Government changed and so did policy;

however, the R34 which had crossed the Atlantic was destroyed in a sudden and violent storm.

Ross's brother Keith died in 1955. Included in his will was a bequest of £100 to WH Shiers, the sole remaining crew member of the England-Australia flight. The Vickers Vimy flown on that occasion is displayed at Adelaide airport. Keith was buried near his brother, father and mother in the North Road Anglican cemetery, Adelaide.

HOWARD FLOREY 1898-1968

DEVELOPER OF PENICILLIN

Howard Florey was born on 24 September at Malvern, South Australia, the son of a boot manufacturer. He was educated at Kyre College and St Peter's College, and was the 1921 University of Adelaide Rhodes Scholar. He and Ernst Chain developed penicillin, the first powerful antibiotic, and the 'silver bullet' which saved millions of human lives by conquering bacterial infection, the most common cause of human death throughout history. Following his lead others developed drugs to treat parasitic diseases and viral infections including AIDS. Australia's longest-serving Prime Minister Robert Menzies said, 'In terms of world well-being, Florey was the most important man ever born in Australia.'

Florey studied physiology under Sir Charles Sherrington and in 1924 moved to Cambridge. He visited the USA for ten months in 1925 and 1926. In 1927 he lectured on the flow of blood and lymph and in 1931 became Professor of Pathology in Sheffield. His grounding in physiology proved useful in this role and he took the pathology chair in the Sir William Dunn School in Oxford in 1935. He studied lysozyme, an antibacterial discovered by Alexander Fleming, and appointed the chemist Ernst Chain to his team. He later selected Fleming's penicillin for this study and conducted successful trials in 1941. He visited Australia in 1944 and had a major role in establishing the Australian National University. Florey was awarded the Nobel Prize for Medicine in 1945, was President of the Royal Society from 1960 to 1965, and in 1965 became Baron Florey of Adelaide and Marston. He has been awarded numerous prestigious awards in many countries.

Although Fleming received most of the credit for the discovery of penicillin, it was Florey who carried out the first ever clinical trial of penicillin in 1941 at the Radcliffe Infirmary in Oxford. The patient started to recover but subsequently died because at that time Florey was unable to make enough penicillin. After scaling up the manufacturing process, Florey and Chain made a useful and effective drug out of penicillin, after the task had been abandoned as too difficult.

Along with the discoveries of Alexander Fleming and Ernst Chain, Florey's discoveries are estimated to have saved over 200 million lives, and he is consequently regarded by the Australian scientific and medical community as one of its greatest figures.

At school Florey excelled in chemistry and physics, but not mathematics. He also played various sports for the school: cricket, football, athletics, and tennis. He studied medicine at the University of Adelaide from 1917 to 1921, paid for entirely by a state scholarship.

Florey continued his studies at Magdalen College, Oxford, as a Rhodes Scholar under the tutelage of Sir Charles Scott Sherrington, receiving the degrees of BA in 1924 and MA in 1935. In 1925, he left Oxford to attend the University of Cambridge, during which time he won a fellowship from the Rockefeller Foundation and studied in the United States for ten months. He returned to England in 1926 and was elected to a fellowship at Gonville and Caius College, Cambridge, and a year later he received the degree of PhD.

After Cambridge, Florey was appointed to the Joseph Hunter Chair of Pathology at the University of Sheffield in 1932. In 1935 he returned to Oxford, as Professor of Pathology and Fellow of Lincoln College, Oxford, leading a team of researchers. Working with Ernst Boris Chain, Norman Heatley and Edward Abraham, he read Alexander Fleming's paper discussing the antibacterial effects of *Penicillium notatum* mould.

In 1941, he and Chain treated their first patient, Albert Alexander, who had had a small sore at the corner of his mouth which then spread, leading to a severe facial infection involving *streptococci* and *staphylococci*. His whole face, eyes and scalp were swollen to the extent that he had had an eye removed to relieve some of the pain. Within a day of being given penicillin, he started recovering. However, the researchers did not have enough penicillin to help him to a full recovery, and he relapsed and died. Because of this experience and of the difficulty in producing penicillin, the researchers changed their focus to children, who could be treated with smaller quantities.

Florey's research team investigated the large-scale production of the mould and efficient extraction of the active ingredient; they succeeded to the point where, by 1945, penicillin production was produced in industrial quantities for the Allies in World War II. However, Florey said that the project was originally driven by scientific interests, and that the medicinal discovery was a bonus:

People sometimes think that I and the others worked on penicillin because we were interested in suffering humanity. I don't think it ever crossed our minds about suffering humanity. This was an interesting scientific exercise, and because it was of some use in medicine is very gratifying, but this was not the reason that we started working on it.

Florey shared the Nobel Prize in Physiology or Medicine in 1945 with Ernst Boris Chain and Alexander Fleming.

In 1958 Florey opened the John Curtin School of Medical Research at ANU in Canberra. In 1965 the Queen made him Lord Florey and he accepted the role of Chancellor of the Australian National University.

On 18 July 1944 Florey was appointed a Knight Bachelor. In 1947 he was awarded the Gold Medal of the Royal Society of Medicine.

He was awarded the Lister Medal in 1945 for his contributions to surgical science. The corresponding Lister Oration, given at the Royal College of Surgeons of England later that year, was titled *Use of Micro-organisms for Therapeutic Purposes*. In 1946, the University of Sao Paulo awarded him an honorary doctorate.

Florey was elected a member of the Royal Society in 1941 and became President in 1958. In 1962, Florey became Provost of The Queen's College, Oxford. During his term as Provost, the college built a new residential block, which was named the Florey Building in his honour. The building was designed by the British architect Sir James Stirling.

On 4 February 1965, Sir Howard was created a life peer and became Baron Florey, of Adelaide in the State of South Australia and Commonwealth of Australia and of Marston in the County of Oxford. This was a higher honour than the knighthood awarded to penicillin's discoverer, Sir Alexander Fleming, and it recognised the monumental work Florey did in making penicillin available in sufficient quantities to save millions of lives in the war, despite Fleming's doubts that this was feasible. On 15 July 1965 Florey was appointed a Member of The Order of Merit.

The lecture theatre at the John Curtin School of Medical Research was named for him during his tenure at the ANU.

Florey's portrait appeared on the Australian $50 note for 22 years (1973–95), and the suburb of Florey in the Australian Capital Territory is named after him. The Florey Institute of Neuroscience and Mental Health, located at the University of Melbourne, Victoria, and a lecture theatre in the University of Adelaide's medical school are also named after him. The defunct Australian Student Prize, given to outstanding high school leavers, was previously called the 'Lord Florey Student Prize' in recognition of Florey.

The Florey Unit of the Royal Berkshire Hospital in Reading, Berkshire, is named after him.

The Florey Institute for Host–Pathogen Interactions at the University of Sheffield is named in his honour.

Howard Florey died of a heart attack in 1968 and was honoured with a memorial service at Westminster Abbey, London.

Penicillin: The Magic Bullet is a 2006 Australian film production written by Gordon Glenn and financed by the Film Finance Corporation and Arcimedia Productions in association with Film Victoria. *Breaking the Mould* is a 2009 historical drama that tells the story of the development of penicillin in the 1930s and 1940s, by the group of scientists at Oxford headed by Florey at the Dunn School of Pathology. The film stars Dominic West as Florey, Denis Lawson, and Oliver Dimsdale; and was written by Kate Brooke and directed by Peter Hoar.

MARK OLIPHANT 1901–2000

PHYSICIST AND GOVERNOR

Markus Laurence Elwin Oliphant was born in Adelaide on 8 October 1901. He was one of the first team to split the atom, showed that hydrogen atoms could fuse (later leading to the invention of the hydrogen bomb), helped develop radar in World War II, was instrumental in arranging the development of the atomic bomb, and later became Governor of South Australia and an advocate for voluntary assisted dying.

Markus was the eldest of five sons. His father was a very religious man and he wanted his eldest son to be a priest, but Oliphant had always been more interested in gadgets and science than in religion. Oliphant was quoted on the Australia Biography website as saying: 'I was always fooling about in the shed at the back of the garden with bits of wire and bits of wood, making what my brothers called my "raggedy, baggedy engines". Still, he was highly influenced by religion as a young man, and he always held a healthy respect for it. As he grew up he also developed an appreciation for education, partly instilled by his mother, who was a schoolteacher. He graduated from high school with good grades before he went on to attend the University of Adelaide. He was originally interested in dentistry or medicine, but his teacher, Dr Roy Burdon, saw an aptitude for physics in the young man and persuaded him to switch his studies. After a short while Oliphant agreed, and he graduated with a degree in physics. To pay for his education he took any odd job he could find, working his way through university.

After graduation he got a job cleaning floors for a jewellery manufacturer. In 1925 he married Rosa Wilbraham, who was also from Adelaide, and they had one daughter. While he was working at the jewellers in 1925, Oliphant attended a lecture given by New Zealand physicist Ernest Rutherford. He was so impressed by what Rutherford had to say that he immediately decided that if he could possibly bring it about, he would work for Rutherford one day. Rutherford worked at the Cavendish Laboratory in Cambridge, England, one of the most advanced research facilities in nuclear physics at that time. In 1927 Oliphant won an exhibition prize at Adelaide University, and then was accepted at Cambridge University.

He took a job as exhibition scholar at the Cavendish Laboratory, fulfilling his wish. He worked there under Rutherford with a team of scientists whose task was to find a way to split an atom. Oliphant and the team he worked with managed to split the first atom in 1932. It was an amazing accomplishment, but did not take up all of Oliphant's time. Besides his work on splitting the atom, Oliphant concentrated on artificially disintegrating the nucleus and positive ions of the atom as well as designing a particle accelerator. While doing these things, Oliphant himself discovered helium 3 and tritium, and also showed that the nuclei of heavy hydrogen could be forced to react with one another and to fuse together. It was this discovery of fusion that led the way to the hydrogen bomb, although Oliphant never wanted nor intended the knowledge to be used in such a way. It was American scientist Edward Teller who used Oliphant's knowledge to build the hydrogen bomb.

In 1937 Oliphant took a position with the University of Birmingham, where he later became Professor of Physics. While at the university in 1939, along with John Randall and Harry Boot he received a grant to help develop a short wavelength radar. It was this radar that helped the fight against the German U-boats and bomber offensives during World War II. Former wavelengths had been around 150 centimetres but these new ones were only 10 centimetres, which meant that the radar waves could be focused in narrow beams on one specific point to find ships, submarines, and aircraft, as well as cities. It was a world-changing discovery. In the same year Oliphant took a trip to visit Berkeley, California. He there met Ernest Lawrence, who taught Oliphant how to build a 60-inch cyclotron. Because of the advent of World War II, he was unable to finish the project until 1950.

In 1940 two men, Otto Frisch and Rudolf Peierls, who also worked at the University of Birmingham, theorised that uranium-235 could be used to create an atom bomb. Oliphant was charged with taking their ideas to a committee, which had the code name of Maud. Maud in turn sent the theory to the United States and its Uranium Committee in March of 1941, but the United States seemed to be uninterested in the idea, as they made no reply to the report. Britain, however, was entrenched in war with Germany and thought the bomb was necessary and important to their efforts. Oliphant was sent to America, where he arranged to meet with the Uranium Committee. He stressed the importance of the project and urged that the Committee begin implementing a plan to develop an atomic weapon. After speaking to the Committee, he went to visit his friends and fellow scientists Ernest Lawrence, James Conant, and Enrico Fermi. He stressed to them the importance of the project, looking to them to back him up.

Because of his efforts, the United States established the Office of Scientific Research and Development. This office took on the Uranium Committee as one of its projects, and in December of 1941, after Pearl Harbor was attacked by the Japanese, they set up the Manhattan Engineering District to house what would soon be called the Manhattan Project, to research the building of a uranium atom bomb. Oliphant moved to America in November of 1943 to work on the Manhattan Project, sent as a British delegate. However, after the use of the atom bomb in 1945 on Hiroshima and Nagasaki, he was appalled by the devastation, and argued against its ever being used again. He especially argued against an American monopoly on nuclear technology. *Time International* wrote that 'Oliphant made key contributions to the understanding of nuclear disintegration and the design of particle accelerators'.

'We had no idea,' he later said, 'that this would one day be applied to make hydrogen bombs.' Although he had been sent to press America to build a bomb, no one at the time knew how devastating such a bomb would be, and Oliphant has said he would not have pressed for its creation if he had known. He did little work on the actual bomb, however, because the idea of it made him anxious; he spent most of his time at Berkeley with Lawrence trying to refine Uranium 235. It was an important project, if less militarily focused. For his work with this he was awarded the Hughes Medal in 1943.

In April 1945 Oliphant returned to England. After VE-Day he returned to the University of Birmingham to continue as Professor of Physics. It was while he was there that he first heard how the atom bomb was used and exactly how powerful it was. He felt justifiably divided about the report. On the one hand he felt a scientist's excitement that an idea he had helped create had worked, but on the other hand, the stronger side, he had a humane abhorrence at what the bomb had cost in human lives. Like so many of the scientists who had worked on the project, Oliphant had never expected that the bomb's effects would be so devastating.

From this point on, Oliphant became an extreme critic of nuclear weapons. He joined the Pugwash Conferences on Science and World Affairs to discuss with people all over the world the idea that no one should ever use such a weapon again. The Economist wrote:

Like many of the scientists who helped to make the atomic bomb,
Mark Oliphant expressed dismay when it was used to destroy

Hiroshima and Nagasaki. During the cold war years he was labelled a 'peacenik', a contemptuous term used to describe those who questioned the morality of using nuclear weapons.

Because of his anti-nuclear weapons stance, Oliphant was often left out of scientific experiments involving nuclear power. The US Government refused to give Oliphant a visa in 1951 when he wanted to attend a nuclear physics conference in Chicago. The British neglected to ask Oliphant for help when they tested 12 nuclear weapons from 1952 to 1957, even though he was exceptionally qualified to assess the safety of the tests to make certain no one was hurt by them. But Oliphant never again changed his opinion on the weapons.

Because of the work he did during the war, Oliphant was given a US Congressional Medal of Freedom with Gold Palm, but the Australian Government vetoed the honour. Oliphant returned to Australia in 1950. There he became the first Director of the Research School of Physical Sciences at the new Australian National University in Canberra. While there, he helped design and build the world's largest homopolar generator, which was used to give power to a large scientific railgun instrument. He also set up the Australian Academy of Science in 1954 and became its first President in 1956. In 1959 Oliphant was knighted.

He retired from the Australian National University in 1967. He was invited to become the Governor of South Australia, which he accepted and held office from 1971 to 1976. As Governor he used his position to oppose France's nuclear testing in the Pacific. He went so far, in fact, that he said he would join anyone putting together an expedition to try to stop them. In 1977 he was made a Companion in the Order of Australia. Oliphant's wife, Rosa, died in 1987. After witnessing her suffering prior to her death, he became a strong proponent for voluntary euthanasia for debilitating and incurable diseases.

Oliphant died in Canberra on 14 July 2000, at the age of 98. Oliphant will not soon be forgotten. Many locations have been named after the great scientist, including the Mark Oliphant Conservation Park, the Oliphant building at Australian National University, the

Oliphant wing of the Physics Building at the University of Adelaide and the Mark Oliphant Building in Bedford Park, South Australia. A South Australian High School science competition was also named in his honour. He will be remembered as the scientist who unwillingly helped to build the atomic bomb, but who stuck by his principles in trying to stop the further development and use of nuclear weapons.

PASTOR NICHOLLS 1906-1988

ATHLETE AND ABORIGINAL
GOVERNOR OF SOUTH AUSTRALIA

Sir Douglas Ralph Nicholls KCVO OBE was a prominent Aboriginal Australian from the Yorta Yorta people. He was a professional athlete, Churches of Christ pastor and ceremonial officer and a pioneering campaigner for cultural reconciliation.

Nicholls was the first Aboriginal Australian to be knighted; he was appointed Knight Bachelor in 1972 and he was appointed a Knight Commander of the Royal Victorian Order in 1977. He was also the first appointed to vice-regal office, serving as Governor of South Australia from 1 December 1976 until his resignation on 30 April 1977 due to poor health.

Nicholls was born on 9 December 1906 on the Cummeragunja Reserve in New South Wales, the youngest of five children born to Herbert Nicholls and Florence Atkinson. His paternal grandfather was Aaron Atkinson, who was the brother of William Cooper.

Schooling at Nicholls' mission was provided to Grade 3 standard and strict religious principles were emphasised. When he was eight, he saw his 16-year-old sister Hilda forcibly taken from his family by the police and taken to the Cootamundra Domestic Training Home for Aboriginal Girls, where she was trained to become a domestic servant.

At 13 Nicholls worked with his uncle as a tar boy and general hand on sheep stations, and he lived with the shearers. He worked hard and had a cheerful disposition. This annoyed one of the shearers so much that he challenged Nicholls to a fight, with the loser to hand over one week's pay (30 shillings – $3). After six rounds the shearer who challenged him conceded defeat.

Nicholls played Australian Rules football. After playing in the Goulburn Valley for Tongala, Nicholls tried out for Victorian Football League (VFL) clubs North Melbourne and Carlton before the 1927 season; he played some seconds matches for Carlton but did not play a senior game. He subsequently joined the Northcote Football Club in the Victorian Football Association (VFA), and became a regular in the Northcote team by 1929. He made his name as an energetic and speedy wingman, capable of spectacular feats, and came to be regarded as the best wingman in the VFA at the time. At 152 cm, he was one of the shortest players in the game. He was a member of Northcote's 1929 premiership team, and finished third in the Recorder Cup voting in 1931, his final season with Northcote.

In 1932, Nicholls joined the VFL's Fitzroy Football Club. In 1934, he was third in the Brownlow Medal count; and in 1935, he was the first Aboriginal player to be selected to play for the Victorian team, ultimately playing four interstate games. He played a total of six seasons for Fitzroy, before returning to Northcote in 1938. Knee injuries forced him to retire in 1939. He returned to Northcote as non-playing coach in 1947.

During his career, particularly in the early years, Nicholls was subjected to onfield taunts or ostracised by his team-mates due to his colour. Nevertheless, he became a popular player among spectators; and, upon joining Fitzroy, when he was initially sitting by himself in the change rooms (due to this ostracism), he was befriended by Haydn Bunton Sr, who ensured he was made welcome within the team.

Like his close relative Lynch Cooper, Nicholls was also a very capable sprinter. He competed in gift races around Victoria during the athletics seasons, and in 1928 he won both the Nyah and Warracknabeal Gifts. Following this, the race organisers paid him an appearance fee, board and expenses to enter races. He was the inaugural Chairman of the National Aboriginal Sports Foundation.

Playing football provided employment during the winter. To earn a living during the rest of the year, he boxed with Jimmy Sharman's Boxing Troupe, a travelling sideshow in which Sharman offered his fighters for challenge against all comers.

During World War II, Nicholls was an adept boomerang thrower, and he taught the skill to some members of the United States military. There is a photograph depicting this in the Australian War Memorial archives. He also organised and captained Aboriginal teams in football matches used for patriotic fundraisers during the war, many of which were played against Northcote.

Nicholls was a minister and social worker with Aboriginal people. Following his mother's death he took a renewed interest in Christianity and was baptised at Northcote Church of Christ (now Northern Community Church of Christ) in 1935. He officiated at church and hymn services as a lay preacher at the Gore Street Mission Centre in Fitzroy.

In 1941 Nicholls received his call-up notice and he joined the 29th Battalion but, in 1942, at the request of the Fitzroy police, he was released from his unit to work as a social worker in the Fitzroy Aboriginal community. He cared for those trapped in alcohol abuse, gambling, and other social problems, and those who were in trouble with the police. Indigenous people gathered to him and eventually the group was so large that he became the pastor of the first Aboriginal Church of Christ in Australia. In recognition of the ministry he was already expressing, he was ordained as a minister.

In a letter to the editor in 1953, it was noted that Opposition Leader, HV Evatt, had asked the Prime Minister Robert Menzies, on 26 February, in Federal Parliament, 'for an invitation to be extended to Capt Reg Saunders or some other outstanding representative of the aborigines' to be included in the official Australian contingent to the coronation of Elizabeth II. The author suggested Nicholls, as an ordained minister, and for his community work in the areas of Fitzroy and Mooroopna.

In 1957 Nicholls became a field officer for the Aborigines Advancement League (AAL). He edited their magazine *Smoke Signals* and helped draw Aboriginal issues to the attention of Government officials and the general public. He pleaded for dignity for Aboriginal people as human beings. Support for the AAL grew rapidly.

Nicholls helped set up hostels for Aboriginal children and holiday homes for Aboriginal people at Queenscliff; he was a founding member and Victorian Secretary of the Federal Council for the Advancement of Aborigines and Torres Strait Islanders (FCAATSI). In response to protests in the 1950s and 60s for an independent, Aboriginal-run farming cooperative at Lake Tyers Mission he campaigned on their behalf, but when the board moved to close Lake Tyers, Nichols resigned his position in protest.

On the nomination of Premier Don Dunstan, he was appointed Governor of South Australia on 1 December 1976. He was the first non-white person to serve as the Governor of an Australian state, and is the only Aboriginal person to have held viceregal office. Because of his race, his nomination proved controversial and attracted more attention than most viceregal appointments. A poll by ABC's *This Day Tonight* found that 70 percent of respondents opposed Nicholls becoming Governor. *The Canberra Times* expressed concern that members of his family might set up camp on the grounds of Government House. However, Adelaide's main daily newspaper *The Advertiser* was more positive, welcoming the news 'without reservation'. News of the appointment was leaked in May 1976, after which he agreed to appear on *A Current Affair*. Nicholls took exception to a question directed at his wife, calling the interviewer a racist and requiring him to leave his house. GTV-9 aired the footage without his permission, and subsequently apologised for doing so.

Nicholls' predecessor as Governor, nuclear physicist Mark Oliphant, confidentially wrote to the State Government expressing concerns about the appointment. He said there were 'grave dangers' involved, as 'there is something inherent in the personality of the Aborigine which makes it difficult for him to adapt fully to the ways of the white man'.

On 25 January 1977, Nicholls suffered a stroke and was admitted to the cardiac ward at Royal Adelaide Hospital. He had a history of high blood pressure and had suffered a mild heart attack some years earlier. He was not discharged until three weeks later, and Lieutenant-Governor Walter Crocker served as Administrator of the Government in his place. Nicholls attended only one further official engagement after his stroke, hosting Queen Elizabeth II at Government House on 20 March. She subsequently awarded him a second knighthood, Knight Commander of the Royal Victorian Order (KCVO). Nicholls' retirement due to ill health was announced on 22 April, with effect from 30 April. He held office for only 150 days, making him the shortest-serving Governor in South Australian history and the only one to serve for less than a year.

In December 1942 Nicholls married Gladys Nicholls, the widow of his brother Howard, who had died in April 1942 as a result of injuries sustained in a car accident. Gladys already had three children. Douglas Nicholls and Gladys were married for 39 years and together raised their combined six children (two sons, Bevan and Ralph, and four daughters, Beryl, Nora, Lilian and Pamela). Lady Gladys Nicholls died in 1981.

Nicholls' great-grandson Nathan Lovett-Murray also played Australian Rules Football, playing 145 games for Essendon.

AWARDS AND ACHIEVEMENTS

1957: Appointed a Member of the Order of the British Empire (MBE).

1962: Chosen by the Father's Day Council of Australia as Victoria's Father of the Year for 'outstanding leadership in youth and welfare work and for the inspired example he set the community in his unfailing efforts to further the cause of the Australian Aborigine'.

1968: Promoted to Officer of the Order of the British Empire (OBE).

1970: Audience with Pope Paul VI in Sydney.

1970: Among Victorian invited guests to greet Queen Elizabeth II on her visit to Australia.

1972: First Aboriginal to be knighted when he was appointed Knight Bachelor and he travelled to London with his wife Gladys to receive the honour.

1973: Appointed King of Moomba.

1976: Appointed the 28th Governor of South Australia, the first Aboriginal person appointed to vice-regal office.

1977: Appointed a Knight Commander of the Royal Victorian Order (KCVO).

1991: The Canberra suburb of Nicholls was named after him.

2001: A new chapel in Preston of the Northern Community Church of Christ, the church in which he was baptised, was named after him.

2006: To commemorate the centenary of his birth, a statue of Nicholls, one-and-a-half times life size, was approved for the Parliament Gardens, beside the Parliament of Victoria; it was officially opened in December 2007 and was the first statue of an Aboriginal erected in Victoria.

2011: Inducted to Victorian Aboriginal Honour Roll.

2016: The AFL named their indigenous round after him and continue to do so.

2018: The federal electoral division of Murray renamed Nicholls in honour of Sir Doug and Lady Nicholls.

2018: A Google Doodle was created to celebrate his 112th birthday.

Nicholls died on 4 June 1988 at Mooroopna. A state funeral was held for him and he was buried in the cemetery at Cummeragunja.

DON BRADMAN 1908-2001

WORLD'S GREATEST TEST
CRICKET BATSMAN

Sir Donald George Bradman AC, often referred to as 'The Don', was an Australian international cricketer and is widely acknowledged as the greatest batsman of all time. Bradman's career Test batting average of 99.94 has been cited as the greatest achievement by any sportsman in any major sport.

It is part of Australian folklore that the young Bradman practised alone with a cricket stump and a golf ball. Bradman's meteoric rise from bush cricket to the Australian Test team took just over two years. Before his 22nd birthday, he had set many records for top scoring, some of which still stand, and became Australia's sporting idol at the height of the Great Depression.

During a 20-year playing career, Bradman consistently scored at a level that made him, in the words of former Australia captain Bill Woodfull, 'worth three batsmen to Australia'. A controversial set of tactics, known as Bodyline, was specifically devised by the England team to curb his scoring. As a captain and administrator, Bradman was committed to attacking, entertaining cricket; he drew spectators in record numbers. He hated the constant adulation, however, and it affected how he dealt with others. The focus of attention on his individual performances strained relationships with some teammates, administrators and journalists, who thought him aloof and wary. Following an enforced hiatus due to the Second World War, he made a dramatic comeback, captaining an Australian team known as 'The Invincibles' on a record-breaking unbeaten tour of England.

A complex, highly driven man, not given to close personal relationships, Bradman retained a pre-eminent position in the game by acting as an administrator, selector and writer for three decades following his retirement. Even after he became reclusive in his declining years, his opinion was highly sought, and his status as a national icon was still recognised. In 1997, almost 50 years after his retirement as a Test player, Prime Minister John Howard of Australia called him the 'greatest living Australian'. Bradman's image has appeared on postage stamps and coins, and a museum dedicated to his life was opened while he was still living. On the centenary of his birth, 27 August 2008, the Royal Australian Mint issued a $5 commemorative gold coin with Bradman's image. In 2009, he was inducted into the ICC Cricket Hall of Fame.

Donald George Bradman was born on 27 August 1908 at Cootamundra, New South Wales. He was the youngest son of George and Emily (née Whatman) Bradman, and he had a brother, Victor, and three sisters, Islet, Lilian and Elizabeth May. While one of his great-grandfathers was one of the first Italians to migrate to Australia in 1826, Bradman was of English heritage on both sides of his family. His grandfather Charles Andrew Bradman came from Withersfield, England. When Bradman played at Cambridge in 1930 as a 21-year-old on his first tour of England, he took the opportunity to trace his forebears in the region.

Bradman's parents lived in the hamlet of Yeo Yeo, near Stockinbingal. His mother Emily gave birth to him at the Cootamundra home of Granny Scholz, a midwife. That house is now the Bradman Birthplace Museum. Emily had hailed from Mittagong in the NSW Southern Highlands, and in 1911, when Don Bradman was about two-and-a-half years old, his parents decided to relocate to Bowral, close to Mittagong, to be closer to Emily's family and friends, as life at Yeo Yeo was proving difficult.

Bradman practised batting incessantly during his youth. He invented his own solo cricket game, using a cricket stump for a bat and a golf ball. A water tank, mounted on a curved brick stand, stood on a paved area behind the family home. When hit into the curved brick facing of the stand, the ball rebounded at high speed and varying angles, and Bradman would attempt to hit it again. This form of practice developed his timing and reactions to a high degree. In more formal cricket, he hit his first century at the age of 12, making an undefeated 115 playing for Bowral Public School against Mittagong High School.

During the 1920–21 season, Bradman acted as scorer for the local Bowral team, captained by his uncle George Whatman. In October 1920, he filled in when the team was one man short, scoring 37 and 29 on debut. During the season, Bradman's father took him to the Sydney Cricket Ground to watch the fifth Ashes Test match. On that day, Bradman formed an ambition: 'I shall never be satisfied,' he told his father, 'until I play on this ground.' Bradman left school in 1922 and went to work for a local real estate agent, who encouraged his sporting pursuits by giving him time off when necessary. He gave up cricket in favour of tennis for two years, but resumed playing cricket in 1925–26.

Bradman became a regular selection for the Bowral team, and several outstanding performances earned him the attention of the Sydney daily press. Competing on matting-over-concrete pitches, Bowral played other rural towns in the Berrima District competition. Bradman made 234 against Wingello, a team that included the future Test bowler Bill O'Reilly. In the competition final against Moss Vale, which extended over five consecutive Saturdays, Bradman scored 320 not out.

During the following Australian winter (1926), an ageing Australian team lost The Ashes in England, and a number of Test players retired. The New South Wales Cricket Association began a hunt for new talent. Mindful of Bradman's big scores for Bowral, the association wrote to him, requesting his attendance at a practice session in Sydney. He was subsequently chosen for the Country Week tournaments at both cricket and tennis, to be played during separate weeks. His boss presented him with an ultimatum: he could have only one week away from work, and therefore had to choose between the two sports. He chose cricket. Bradman's performances during Country Week resulted in an invitation to play grade cricket in Sydney for St George in the 1926–27 season. He scored 110 on his debut, making his first century on a turf wicket. On 1 January 1927, he turned out for the NSW second team. For the remainder of the season, Bradman travelled the 130 kilometres from Bowral to Sydney every Saturday to play for St George.

The next season continued the rapid rise of the 'Boy from Bowral'. Selected to replace the unfit Archie Jackson in the NSW team, Bradman made his first-class debut at the Adelaide Oval, aged 19. He secured the achievement of a hundred on debut, with an innings of 118 featuring what soon became his trademarks – fast footwork, calm confidence and rapid scoring. In the final match of the season, he made his first century at the SCG, against the Sheffield Shield champions Victoria. Despite his potential, Bradman was not chosen for the Australian second team to tour New Zealand.

Bradman decided that his chances for Test selection would be improved by moving to Sydney for the 1928–29 season, when England were to tour in defence of the Ashes. Initially, he continued working in real estate, but later took a promotions job with the sporting goods retailer Mick Simmons Ltd. In the first match of the Sheffield Shield season, he scored a century in each innings against Queensland. He followed this with scores of 87 and 132 not out against the England touring team, and was rewarded with selection for the first Test, to be played at Brisbane.

Playing in only his tenth first-class match, Bradman, nicknamed 'Braddles' by his teammates, found his initial Test a harsh learning experience. Caught on a sticky wicket, Australia were all out for 66 in the second innings and lost by 675 runs (still a Test record). Following scores of 18 and 1, the selectors dropped Bradman to twelfth man for the Second Test. An injury to Bill Ponsford early in the match required Bradman to field as substitute while England amassed 636, following their 863 runs in the First Test. RS 'Dick' Whitington wrote, '... he had scored only nineteen himself and these experiences appear to have provided him with food for thought'. Recalled for the Third Test at the Melbourne Cricket Ground, Bradman scored 79 and 112 to become the youngest player to make a Test century, although the match was still lost. Another loss followed in the Fourth Test. Bradman reached 58 in the second innings and appeared set to guide the team to victory when he was run out. It was to be the only run out of his Test career. The losing margin was just 12 runs.

The improving Australians did manage to win the Fifth and final Test. Bradman top-scored with 123 in the first innings, and was at the wicket in the second innings when his Captain, Jack Ryder, hit the winning runs. Bradman completed the season with 1,690 first-class runs, averaging 93.88; and his first multiple century in a Sheffield Shield match, 340 not out against Victoria, set a new ground record for the SCG. Bradman averaged 113.28 in 1929–30. In a trial match to select the team that would tour England, he was last man out in the first innings for 124. As his team followed on, the skipper Bill Woodfull asked Bradman to keep the pads on and open the second innings. By the end of play, he was 205 not out, on his way to 225. Against Queensland at the SCG, Bradman set a then world record for first-class cricket by scoring 452 not out; he made his runs in only 415 minutes. Not long after the feat, he recalled:

On 434...I had a curious intuition...I seemed to sense that the ball would be a short-pitched one on the leg-stump, and I could almost feel myself getting ready to make my shot before the ball was delivered. Sure enough, it pitched exactly where I had anticipated, and, hooking it to the square-leg boundary, I established the only record upon which I had set my heart.

Although he was an obvious selection to tour England, Bradman's unorthodox style raised doubts that he could succeed on the slower English pitches. Percy Fender wrote:

...he will always be in the category of the brilliant, if unsound, ones. Promise there is in Bradman in plenty, though watching him does not inspire one with any confidence that he desires to take the only course which will lead him to a fulfilment of that promise. He makes a mistake, then makes it again and again; he does not correct it, or look as if he were trying to do so. He seems to live for the exuberance of the moment.

The encomiums were not confined to his batting gifts; nor did the criticism extend to his character. 'Australia has unearthed a champion,' said former Australian Test great Clem Hill, 'self-taught, with natural ability. But most important of all, with his heart in the right place.' Selector Dick Jones weighed in with the observation that it was 'good to watch him talking to an old player, listening attentively to everything that is said and then replying with a modest 'thank you''.

England were favourites to win the 1930 Ashes series, and if the Australians were to exceed expectations, their young batsmen, Bradman and Jackson, needed to prosper. With his elegant batting technique, Jackson appeared the brighter prospect of the pair. However, Bradman began the tour with 236 at Worcester and went on to score 1,000 first-class runs by the end of May, the fifth player (and first Australian) to achieve this rare feat. In his first Test appearance in England, Bradman hit 131 in the second innings, but England won the match. His batting reached a new level in the Second Test at Lord's where he scored 254 as Australia won and levelled the series. Later in life, Bradman rated this the best innings of his career, as 'practically without exception every ball went where it was intended to go'. *Wisden* noted his fast footwork and how he hit the ball 'all round the wicket with power and accuracy', as well as faultless concentration in keeping the ball on the ground.

In terms of runs scored, this performance was soon surpassed. In the Third Test, at Headingley, Bradman scored a century before lunch on 11 July, the first day of the Test match, to equal the performances of Victor Trumper and Charlie McCartney. In the afternoon, Bradman added another century between lunch and tea, before finishing the day on 309 not out. He remains the only Test player to pass 300 in one day's play. His eventual score of 334 was a world record, exceeding the previous mark of 325 by Andy Sandham. Bradman dominated the Australian innings; the second-highest tally was 77 by Alan Kippax. Businessman Arthur Whitelaw later presented Bradman with a cheque for £1,000 in appreciation of his achievement. The match ended in anti-climax as poor weather prevented a result, as it also did in the Fourth Test.

In the deciding Test at The Oval, England made 405. During an innings stretching over three days due to intermittent rain, Bradman made yet another multiple century, this time 232, which helped give Australia a big lead of 290 runs. In a crucial partnership with Archie Jackson, Bradman battled through a difficult session when England fast bowler Harold Larwood bowled short on a pitch enlivened by the rain. *Wisden* gave this period of play only a passing mention:

> *On the Wednesday morning the ball flew about a good deal, both batsmen frequently being hit on the body...on more than one occasion each player cocked the ball up dangerously but always, as it happened, just wide of the fieldsmen.*

A number of English players and commentators noted Bradman's discomfort in playing the short, rising delivery. The revelation came too late for this particular match, but was to have immense significance in the next Ashes series. Australia won the match by an innings and regained the Ashes. The victory made an impact in Australia. With the economy sliding toward depression and unemployment rapidly rising, the country found solace in sporting triumph. The story of a self-taught 22-year-old from the bush who set a series of records against the old rival made Bradman a national hero. The statistics Bradman achieved on the tour, and in the Test matches in particular, broke records for the day and some have stood the test of time. In all, Bradman scored 974 runs at an average of 139.14 during the Test series, with four centuries, including two double hundreds and a triple. As of 2018, no one has matched or exceeded 974 runs or three double centuries in one Test series; the record of 974 runs exceeds the second-best performance by 69 runs and was achieved in two fewer innings. Bradman's first-class tally, 2,960 runs (at an average of 98.66 with 10 centuries), was another enduring record: the most by any overseas batsman on a tour of England.

On the tour, the dynamic nature of Bradman's batting contrasted sharply with his quiet, solitary off-field demeanour. He was described as aloof from his teammates and he did not offer to buy them a round of drinks, let alone share the money given to him by Whitelaw. Bradman spent a lot of his free time alone, writing, as he had sold the rights to a book. On his return to Australia, Bradman was surprised by the intensity of his reception, and he became a 'reluctant hero'. Mick Simmons wanted to cash in on their employee's newly won fame. They asked Bradman to leave his teammates and attend official receptions they organised in Adelaide, Melbourne, Goulburn, his hometown Bowral and Sydney, where he received a brand new custom-built Chevrolet. At each stop, Bradman received a level of adulation that 'embarrassed' him. This focus on individual accomplishment in a team game '... permanently damaged relationships with his contemporaries'. Commenting on Australia's victory, the team's Vice-Captain Vic Richardson said: '... we could have played any team without Bradman, but we could not have played the blind school without Clarrie Grimmett.' A modest Bradman can be heard in a 1930 recording saying: 'I have always endeavoured to do my best for the side, and the few centuries that have come my way have been achieved in the hope of winning matches. My one idea when going into bat was to make runs for Australia.'

In 1930–31, against the first West Indian side to visit Australia, Bradman's scoring was more sedate than in England, although he did make 223 in 297 minutes in the Third Test at Brisbane and 152 in 154 minutes in the following Test at Melbourne. However, he scored quickly in a very successful sequence of innings against the South Africans in the Australian summer of 1931–32. For NSW against the tourists, he made 30, 135 and 219. In the Test matches, he scored 226 (277 minutes), 112 (155 minutes), 2 and 167 (183 minutes); his 299 not out in the Fourth Test, at Adelaide, set a new record for the highest score in a Test in Australia. Australia won nine of the ten Tests played over the two series.

At this point, Bradman had played 15 Test matches since the beginning of 1930, scoring 2,227 runs at an average of 131. He had played 18 innings, scoring 10 centuries, six of which had extended beyond 200. His overall scoring rate was 42 runs per hour, with 856 (or 38.5% of his tally) scored in boundaries. Significantly, he had not hit a six, which typified Bradman's attitude: if he hit the ball along the ground, then it could not be caught. During this phase of his career, his youth and natural fitness allowed him to adopt a 'machine-like' approach to batting. The South African fast bowler Sandy Bell described bowling to him as 'heart-breaking … with his sort of cynical grin, which rather reminds one of the Sphinx … he never seems to perspire'.

Between these two seasons, Bradman seriously contemplated playing professional cricket in England with the Lancashire League club Accrington, a move that, according to the rules of the day, would have ended his Test career. A consortium of three Sydney businesses offered an alternative. They devised a two-year contract whereby Bradman wrote for Associated Newspapers, broadcast on Radio 2UE and promoted the menswear retailing chain FJ Palmer and Son. However, the contract increased Bradman's dependence on his public profile, making it more difficult to maintain the privacy that he ardently desired.

Bradman's chaotic wedding to Jessie Menzies in April 1932 epitomised these new and unwelcome intrusions into his private life. The church 'was under siege all throughout the day ... uninvited guests stood on chairs and pews to get a better view'; police erected barriers that were broken down and many of those invited could not get a seat. Just weeks later, Bradman joined a private team organised by Arthur Mailey to tour the United States and Canada. He travelled with his wife, and the couple treated the trip as a honeymoon. Playing 51 games in 75 days, Bradman scored 3,779 runs at 102.1, with 18 centuries. Although the standard of play was not high, the effects of the amount of cricket Bradman had played in the three previous years, together with the strains of his celebrity status, began to show on his return home.

Within the Marylebone Cricket Club (MCC), which administered English cricket at the time, few voices were more influential than that of 'Plum' Warner who, when considering England's response to Bradman, wrote that it 'must evolve a new type of bowler and develop fresh ideas and strange tactics to curb his almost uncanny skill'. To that end, Warner orchestrated the appointment of Douglas Jardine as England captain in 1931, as a prelude to Jardine leading the 1932–33 tour to Australia, with Warner as team manager. Remembering that Bradman had struggled against bouncers during his 232 at The Oval in 1930, Jardine decided to combine traditional leg theory with short-pitched bowling to combat Bradman. He settled on the Nottinghamshire fast bowlers Harold Larwood and Bill Voce as the spearheads for his tactics. In support, the England selectors chose another three pacemen for the squad. The unusually high number of fast bowlers caused a lot of comment in both countries and roused Bradman's own suspicions.

Bradman had other problems to deal with at this time; among these were bouts of illness from an undiagnosed malaise which had begun during the tour of North America, and the initial refusal of the Australian Board of Control to give him permission to write a column for the *Sydney Sun*. Bradman, who had signed a two-year contract with the newspaper, threatened to withdraw from cricket to honour his contract when the Board denied him permission to write; eventually, the paper released Bradman from the contract, in a victory for the Board. In three first-class games against England before the Tests, Bradman averaged just 17.16 in 6 innings. Jardine decided to give the new tactics a trial in only one game, a fixture against an Australian XI at Melbourne. In this match, Bradman faced the leg theory and later warned local administrators that trouble was brewing if it continued. He withdrew from the First Test at the Sydney Cricket Ground amid rumours that he had suffered a nervous breakdown. Despite his absence, England employed what were already becoming known as the Bodyline tactics against the Australian batsmen and won an ill-tempered match.

The public clamoured for the return of Bradman to defeat Bodyline: 'he was the batsman who could conquer this cankerous bowling ... "Bradmania", amounting almost to religious fervour, demanded his return'. Bradman recovered from his indisposition and returned to the side in Alan Kippax's position. A world record crowd of 63,993 at the MCG saw Bradman come to the crease on the first day of the Second Test with the score at 2/67. A standing ovation ensued that delayed play for several minutes. Bradman anticipated receiving a bouncer as his first ball and, as the bowler delivered, he moved across his stumps to play the hook shot. The ball failed to rise and Bradman dragged it onto his stumps; the first-ball duck was his first in a Test. The crowd fell into stunned silence as he walked off. However, Australia took a first innings lead in the match, and another record crowd on 2 January 1933 watched Bradman hit a counter-attacking second innings century. His unbeaten 103 (from 146 balls) in a team total of 191 helped set England a target of 251 to win. Bill O'Reilly and Bert Ironmonger bowled Australia to a series-levelling victory amid hopes that Bodyline was beaten.

The Third Test at the Adelaide Oval proved pivotal. There were angry crowd scenes after the Australian Captain Bill Woodfull and wicket-keeper Bert Oldfield were hit by bouncers. An apologetic Plum Warner entered the Australian dressing room and was rebuked by Woodfull. Woodfull's remarks, that '...there are two teams out there and only one of them is playing cricket', were leaked to the press. Warner and others attributed this to Australian opening batsman Jack Fingleton, but for many years (even after Fingleton's death) a bitter war of accusation passed between Fingleton and Bradman as to who was the real source of the leak. In a cable to the MCC, the Australian Board of Control repeated the allegation of poor sportsmanship directed at Warner by Woodfull.

With the support of the MCC, England continued with Bodyline despite Australian protests. The tourists won the last three Tests convincingly and regained the Ashes. Bradman caused controversy with his own tactics. Always seeking to score, and with the leg side packed with fielders, he often backed away and hit the ball into the vacant half of the outfield with unorthodox shots reminiscent of tennis or golf. This brought him 396 runs (at 56.57) for the series and plaudits for attempting to find a solution to Bodyline, although his series average was just 57% of his career mean. Jack Fingleton was in no doubt that Bradman's game altered irrevocably as a consequence of Bodyline, writing:

> *Bodyline was specially prepared, nurtured for and expended on him and, in consequence, his technique underwent a change quicker than might have been the case with the passage of time. Bodyline plucked something vibrant from his art.*

The constant glare of celebrity and the tribulations of the season forced Bradman to reappraise his life outside the game and to seek a career away from his cricketing fame. Harry Hodgetts, a South Australian delegate to the Board of Control, offered Bradman work as a stockbroker if he would relocate to Adelaide and captain South Australia (SA). Unknown to the public, the SA Cricket Association (SACA) instigated Hodgetts' approach and subsidised Bradman's wage. Although his wife was hesitant about moving, Bradman eventually agreed to the deal in February 1934.

In his farewell season for NSW, Bradman averaged 132.44, his best yet. He was appointed Vice-Captain for the 1934 tour of England. However, 'he was unwell for much of the [English] summer, and reports in newspapers hinted that he was suffering from heart trouble'.

Although he again started with a double century at Worcester, his famed concentration soon deserted him. *Wisden* wrote:

...there were many occasions on which he was out to wild strokes. Indeed at one period he created the impression that, to some extent, he had lost control of himself and went in to bat with an almost complete disregard for anything in the shape of a defensive stroke.

At one stage, Bradman went 13 first-class innings without a century, the longest such spell of his career, prompting suggestions that Bodyline had eroded his confidence and altered his technique. After three Tests, the series was one-one and Bradman had scored 133 runs in five innings. The Australians travelled to Sheffield and played a warm up game before the Fourth Test. Bradman started slowly and then, '... the old Bradman [was] back with us, in the twinkling of an eye, almost'. He went on to make 140, with the last 90 runs coming in just 45 minutes. On the opening day of the Fourth Test at Headingley (Leeds), England were out for 200, but Australia slumped to 3/39, losing the third wicket from the last ball of the day. Listed to bat at number five, Bradman was to start his innings the next day.

That evening, Bradman declined an invitation to dinner from Neville Cardus, telling the journalist that he wanted an early night because the team needed him to make a double century the next day. Cardus pointed out that his previous innings on the ground was 334, and the law of averages was against another such score. Bradman told Cardus, 'I don't believe in the law of averages.' In the event, Bradman batted all of the second day and into the third, putting on a then world record partnership of 388 with Bill Ponsford. When he was finally out for 304 (473 balls, 43 fours and 2 sixes), Australia had a lead of 350 runs, but rain prevented them from forcing a victory. The effort of the lengthy innings stretched Bradman's reserves of energy, and he did not play again until the Fifth Test at The Oval, the match that would decide the Ashes.

In the first innings at The Oval, Bradman and Ponsford recorded an even more massive partnership, this time 451 runs. It had taken them less than a month to break the record they had set at Headingley; this new world record was to last 57 years. Bradman's share of the stand was 244 from 271 balls, and the Australian total of 701 set up victory by 562 runs. For the fourth time in five series, the Ashes changed hands. England would not recover them again until after Bradman's retirement.

Seemingly restored to full health, Bradman blazed two centuries in the last two games of the tour. However, when he returned to London to prepare for the trip home, he experienced severe abdominal pain. It took a doctor more than 24 hours to diagnose acute appendicitis and a surgeon operated immediately. Bradman lost a lot of blood during the four-hour procedure and peritonitis set in. Penicillin and sulphonamides were still experimental treatments at this time, and peritonitis was usually a fatal condition. On 25 September, the hospital issued a statement that Bradman was struggling for his life and that blood donors were needed urgently.

The effect of the announcement was 'little short of spectacular'. The hospital could not deal with the number of donors and closed its switchboard in the face of the avalanche of telephone calls generated by the news. Journalists were asked by their editors to prepare obituaries. Teammate Bill O'Reilly took a call from King George V's Secretary asking that the King be kept informed of the situation. Jessie Bradman started the month-long journey to London as soon as she received the news. En route, she heard a rumour that her husband had died. A telephone call clarified the situation and by the time she reached London, Bradman had begun a slow recovery. He followed medical advice to convalesce, taking several months to return to Australia and missing the 1934–35 Australian season.

There was off-field intrigue in Australian cricket during the antipodean winter of 1935. Australia, scheduled to make a tour of South Africa at the end of the year, needed to replace the retired Bill Woodfull as Captain. The Board of Control wanted Bradman to lead the team, but on 8 August, they announced Bradman's withdrawal from the team due to a lack of fitness. Surprisingly, in the light of this announcement, Bradman led the South Australian team in a full programme of matches that season.

The captaincy was given to Vic Richardson, Bradman's predecessor as South Australian Captain. Cricket author Chris Harte's analysis of the situation is that a prior (unspecified) commercial agreement forced Bradman to remain in Australia. Harte attributed an ulterior motive to his relocation: the off-field behaviour of Richardson and other South Australian players had displeased the South Australia Cricket Association (SACA), which was looking for new leadership. To help improve discipline, Bradman became a committeeman of the SACA, and a selector of the South Australian and Australian teams. He took his adopted state to its first Sheffield Shield title for 10 years, Bradman weighing in with personal contributions of 233 against Queensland and 357 against Victoria. He finished the season with 369 (in 233 minutes), a South Australian record, made against Tasmania. The bowler who dismissed him, Reginald Townley, later became leader of the Tasmanian Liberal Party.

Australia defeated South Africa 4–0 and senior players such as Bill O'Reilly were pointed in their comments about the enjoyment of playing under Richardson's captaincy. A group of players who were openly hostile toward Bradman formed during the tour. For some, the prospect of playing under Bradman was daunting, as was the knowledge that he would additionally be sitting in judgement of their abilities in his role as a selector.

To start the new season, the Test side played a 'Rest of Australia' team, captained by Bradman, at Sydney in early October 1936. The Test XI suffered a big defeat, due to Bradman's 212 and a haul of 12 wickets taken by leg-spinner Frank Ward. Bradman let the members of the Test team know that despite their recent success, the team still required improvement. Shortly afterwards, Bradman's first child was born on 28 October, but died the next day. He took time out of cricket for two weeks and on his return made 192 in three hours against Victoria in the last match before the beginning of the Ashes series.

The Test selectors made five changes to the team who had played in the previous Test match. Significantly, Australia's most successful bowler, Clarrie Grimmett, was replaced by Ward, one of four players making their debut. Bradman's role in Grimmett's omission from the team was controversial and it became a theme that dogged Bradman as Grimmett continued to be prolific in domestic cricket while his successors were ineffective – he was regarded as having finished the veteran bowler's Test career in a political purge. The five Tests drew more than 950,000 spectators including a world record 350,534 to the Third Test at Melbourne.

Australia fell to successive defeats in the opening two Tests; Bradman made two ducks in his four innings, and it seemed that the captaincy was affecting his form. The selectors made another four changes to the team for the Third Test at Melbourne.

Bradman won the toss on New Year's Day 1937, but again failed with the bat, scoring just 13. The Australians could not take advantage of a pitch that favoured batting, and finished the day at 6/181. On the second day, rain dramatically altered the course of the game. With the sun drying the pitch (in those days, covers could not be used during matches) Bradman declared to get England in to bat while the pitch was 'sticky'; England also declared to get Australia back in, conceding a lead of 124. Bradman countered by reversing his batting order to protect his run-makers while conditions improved. The ploy worked and Bradman went in at number seven. In an innings spread over three days, he battled influenza while scoring 270 off 375 balls, sharing a record partnership of 346 with Jack Fingleton, and Australia went on to victory. In 2001, *Wisden* rated this performance as the best Test match innings of all time.

The next Test, at the Adelaide Oval, was fairly even until Bradman played another patient second innings, making 212 from 395 balls. Australia levelled the series when the erratic left-arm spinner 'Chuck' Fleetwood-Smith bowled Australia to victory. In the series-deciding Fifth Test, Bradman returned to a more aggressive style in top-scoring with 169 (off 191 balls) in Australia's 604 and Australia won by an innings. Australia's achievement of winning a Test series after outright losses in the first two matches has never been repeated in Test cricket.

Bradman played the most consistent cricket of his career during the 1938 tour of England. He needed to score heavily as England had a strengthened batting line-up, while the Australian bowling was over-reliant on O'Reilly. Grimmett was overlooked, but Jack Fingleton made the team, so the clique of anti-Bradman players remained. Playing 26 innings on tour, Bradman recorded 13 centuries (a new Australian record) and again made 1,000 first-class runs before the end of May, becoming the only player to do so twice. In scoring 2,429 runs, Bradman achieved the highest average ever recorded in an English season: 115.66.

In the First Test, England amassed a big first innings score and looked likely to win, but Stan McCabe made 232 for Australia, a performance Bradman rated as the best he had ever seen. With Australia forced to follow-on, Bradman fought hard to ensure McCabe's effort was not in vain, and he secured the draw with 144 not out. It was the slowest Test hundred of his career and he played a similar innings of 102 not out in the next Test as Australia struggled to another draw. Rain completely washed out the Third Test at Old Trafford.

Australia's opportunity came at Headingley, a Test described by Bradman as the best he ever played in. England batted first and made 223. During the Australian innings, Bradman backed himself by opting to bat on in poor light conditions, reasoning that Australia could score more runs in bad light on a good wicket than on a rain-affected wicket in good light, when he had the option to go off. He scored 103 out of a total of 242 and the gamble paid off, as it meant there was sufficient time to push for victory when an England collapse left them a target of only 107 to win. Australia slumped to 4/61, with Bradman out for 16. An approaching storm threatened to wash the game out, but the poor weather held off and Australia managed to secure the win, a victory that retained the Ashes. For the only time in his life, the tension of the occasion got to Bradman and he could not watch the closing stages of play, a reflection of the pressure that he had felt all tour: he described the captaincy as 'exhausting' and said he 'found it difficult to keep going'.

The euphoria of securing the Ashes preceded Australia's heaviest defeat. At The Oval, England amassed a world record of 7/903 and their opening batsman Len Hutton scored an individual world record, by making 364. In an attempt to relieve the burden on his bowlers, Bradman took a rare turn at bowling. During his third over, he fractured his ankle and teammates carried him from the ground. With Bradman injured and Fingleton unable to bat because of a leg muscle strain, Australia were thrashed by an innings and 579 runs, which remains the largest margin in Test cricket history. Unfit to complete the tour, Bradman left the team in the hands of Vice-Captain Stan McCabe. At this point, Bradman felt that the burden of captaincy would prevent him from touring England again, although he did not make his doubts public.

Despite the pressure of captaincy, Bradman's batting form remained supreme. An experienced, mature player now commonly called 'The Don' had replaced the blitzing style of his early days as the 'Boy from Bowral'. In 1938–39, he led South Australia to the Sheffield Shield and made a century in six consecutive innings to equal CB Fry's world record. Bradman totalled 21 first-class centuries in 34 innings, from the beginning of the 1938 tour of England (including preliminary games in Australia) until early 1939.

The next season, Bradman made an abortive bid to join the Victoria state side. The Melbourne Cricket Club advertised the position of Club Secretary and he was led to believe that if he applied, he would get the job. The position, which had been held by Hugh Trumble until his death in August 1938, was one of the most prestigious jobs in Australian cricket. The annual salary of £1,000 would make Bradman financially secure while allowing him to retain a connection with the game. On 18 January 1939, the Club's Committee, on the casting vote of the Chairman, chose former Test batsman Vernon Ransford over Bradman.

The 1939–40 season was Bradman's most productive ever for SA: 1,448 runs at an average of 144.8. He made three double centuries, including 251 not out against NSW; he rated the innings as the best he ever played in the Sheffield Shield, as he tamed Bill O'Reilly at the height of his form. However, it was the end of an era. The outbreak of World War II led to the indefinite postponement of all cricket tours, and the suspension of the Sheffield Shield competition.

Bradman joined the Royal Australian Air Force (RAAF) on 28 June 1940 and was passed fit for air crew duty. The RAAF had more recruits than it could equip and train, and Bradman spent four months in Adelaide before the Governor-General of Australia, Lord Gowrie, persuaded Bradman to transfer to the Army, a move that was criticised as a safer option for him. Given the rank of Lieutenant, he was posted to the Army School of Physical Training at Frankston, Victoria, to act as a divisional supervisor of physical training. The exertion of the job aggravated his chronic muscular problems, diagnosed as fibrositis. Surprisingly, in light of his batting prowess, a routine army test revealed that Bradman had poor eyesight.

Invalided out of service in June 1941, Bradman spent months recuperating, unable even to shave himself or comb his hair due to the extent of the muscular pain he suffered. He resumed stock-broking during 1942. In his biography of Bradman, Charles Williams expounded the theory that the physical problems were psychosomatic, induced by stress and possibly depression; Bradman read the book's manuscript and did not disagree. Had any cricket been played at this time, he would not have been available. Although he found some relief in 1945 when referred to the Melbourne masseur Ern Saunders, Bradman permanently lost the feeling in the thumb and index finger of his (dominant) right hand.

In June 1945, Bradman faced a financial crisis when the firm of Harry Hodgetts collapsed due to fraud and embezzlement. Bradman moved quickly to set up his own business, utilising Hodgetts' client list and his old office in Grenfell Street, Adelaide. The fallout led to a prison term for Hodgetts, and left a stigma attached to Bradman's name in the city's business community for many years.

However, the SA Cricket Association had no hesitation in appointing Bradman as their delegate to the Board of Control in place of Hodgetts. Now working alongside some of the men he had battled in the 1930s, Bradman quickly became a leading light in the administration of the game. With the resumption of international cricket, he was once more appointed a Test selector, and played a major role in planning for post-war cricket.

In 1945–46, Bradman suffered regular bouts of fibrositis while coming to terms with increased administrative duties and the establishment of his business. He played for South Australia in two matches to help with the re-establishment of first-class cricket and later described his batting as 'painstaking'. Batting against the Australian Services cricket team, Bradman scored 112 in less than two hours, yet Dick Whitington (playing for the Services) wrote, 'I have seen today the ghost of a once great cricketer.' Bradman declined a tour of New Zealand and spent the winter of 1946 wondering whether he had played his last match. With the English team due to arrive for the 1946–47 Ashes series, the media and the public 'were anxious to know if Bradman would lead Australia'. His doctor recommended against a return to the game. Encouraged by his wife, Bradman agreed to play in lead-up fixtures to the Test series. After hitting two centuries, Bradman made himself available for the First Test at The Gabba.

Controversy emerged on the first day of the First Test at Brisbane. After compiling an uneasy 28 runs, Bradman hit a ball to the gully fieldsman, Jack Ikin. An appeal for a catch was denied in the umpire's contentious ruling that 'it was a bump ball'. At the end of the over, England Captain Wally Hammond spoke with Bradman and criticised him for not 'walking'. 'From then on,' Whitington wrote, 'the series was a cricketing war just when most people desired peace.'

Bradman regained his finest pre-war form in making 187, followed by 234 during the Second Test at Sydney (Sid Barnes also scored 234 during the innings, many in a still standing 405 run 5th Wicket partnership with Bradman; Barnes later recalled that he purposely got out on 234 because 'it wouldn't be right for someone to make more runs than Bradman'). Australia won both matches by an innings. Jack Fingleton speculated that had the decision at Brisbane gone against him, Bradman would have retired, such were his fitness problems. In the remainder of the series, Bradman made three half-centuries in six innings, but was unable to make another century; nevertheless, his team won handsomely, 3-0. He was the leading batsman on either side, with an average of 97.14. Nearly 850,000 spectators watched the Tests, which helped lift public spirits after the war.

India made its first tour of Australia in the 1947–48 season. On 15 November, Bradman made 172 against them for an Australian XI at Sydney, his 100th first-class century. The first non-Englishman to achieve the milestone, Bradman remains the only Australian to have done so. In five tests, he scored 715 runs (at 178.75 average). His last double century (201) came at Adelaide, and he scored a century in each innings of the Melbourne Test. On the eve of the Fifth Test, he announced that the match would be his last in Australia, although he would tour England as a farewell.

Australia had assembled one of the great teams of cricket history. Bradman made it known that he wanted to go through the tour unbeaten, a feat never before accomplished. English spectators were drawn to the matches knowing that it would be their last opportunity to see Bradman in action. RC Robertson-Glasgow observed of Bradman that:

Next to Mr. Winston Churchill, he was the most celebrated man in England during the summer of 1948. His appearances throughout the country were like one continuous farewell matinée.

At last his batting showed human fallibility. Often, especially at the start of the innings, he played where the ball wasn't, and spectators rubbed their eyes.

Despite his waning powers, Bradman compiled 11 centuries on the tour, amassing 2,428 runs (average 89.92). His highest score of the tour (187) came against Essex, when Australia compiled a world record of 721 runs in a day. In the Tests, he scored a century at Trent Bridge, but the performance most like his pre-war exploits came in the Fourth Test at Headingley. England declared on the last morning of the game, setting Australia a world record 404 runs to win in only 345 minutes on a heavily worn wicket. In partnership with Arthur Morris(182), Bradman reeled off 173 not out and the match was won with 15 minutes to spare. The journalist Ray Robinson called the victory 'the finest ever in its conquest of seemingly insuperable odds'.

In the final Test at The Oval, Bradman walked out to bat in Australia's first innings. He received a standing ovation from the crowd and three cheers from the opposition. His Test batting average stood at 101.39. Facing the wrist-spin of Eric Hollies, Bradman pushed forward to the second ball that he faced, was deceived by a googly, and bowled between bat and pad for a duck. An England batting collapse resulted in an innings defeat, denying Bradman the opportunity to bat again and so his career average finished at 99.94; if he had scored just four runs in his last innings, it would have been 100. A story developed over the years that claimed Bradman missed the ball because of tears in his eyes, a claim Bradman denied for the rest of his life.

The Australian team won the Ashes 4-0, completed the tour unbeaten, and entered history as The Invincibles. Just as Bradman's legend grew, rather than diminished, over the years, so too has the reputation of the 1948 team. For Bradman, it was the most personally fulfilling period of his playing days, as the divisiveness of the 1930s had passed. He wrote:

Knowing the personnel, I was confident that here at last was the great opportunity which I had longed for. A team of cricketers whose respect and loyalty were unquestioned, who would regard me in a fatherly sense and listen to my advice, follow my guidance and not question my handling of affairs...there are no longer any fears that they will query the wisdom of what you do. The result is a sense of freedom to give full reign to your own creative ability and personal judgment.

With Bradman retired from professional cricket, RC Robertson-Glasgow wrote of the English reaction: '... a miracle has been removed from among us. So must ancient Italy have felt when she heard of the death of Hannibal'.

TOM KRUSE 1914–2011

OUTBACK MAILMAN

Esmond Gerald (Tom) Kruse MBE was a mail carrier on the Birdsville Track in the border area between South Australia and Queensland. He became known via John Heyer's film *The Back of Beyond*, winner of the Grand Prix Absolute at the 1954 Venice Film Festival. In the 1955 British New Year Honours List, Kruse was appointed Member of the Order of the British Empire (MBE) for services to the community in the outback.

Kruse was born at Waterloo in South Australia to Harry (Heinrich) and Ida Kruse. He was the tenth of their twelve children. He left school when he was 14 years old, and worked as a casual labourer on local farms. However, due to the Depression, he 'went bush' in around 1934 to work in John Penna's haulage business which ran out of Yunta in the mid-north of South Australia.

Kruse married Audrey Valma Fuller (known as Val) on 24 January 1942 in Adelaide, South Australia. They had four children: Pauline, Helen, Phillip and Jeffery.

In 1936 Henry Edgar (Harry) Ding (1907–1976) bought the mail contract from John Penna, and Kruse began his first run on 1 January in that year. Kruse bought the mail contract in 1947 and sold it in 1963.

Kruse worked the Birdsville Track mail run from 1936 to 1957, driving his Leyland Badger truck. He delivered mail and other supplies including general stores, fuel and medicine to remote stations from Marree in north-west South Australia to Birdsville in central Queensland, some 325 miles (523 kilometres) away. Each trip would take two weeks and Tom regularly had to manage breakdowns, flooding creeks and rivers, and getting bogged in desert dunes.

John Heyer's documentary *The Back of Beyond* follows a 'typical' journey made by Kruse, showing the various people he met along the Track and the sorts of obstacles he faced. This particular journey was closely scripted and includes a number of re-enactments and a story about lost children. John Heyer had undertaken a research trip with Kruse earlier, and shooting on the film, using the Badger truck, began in late 1952.

Kruse abandoned the truck on Pandie Pandie Station near Birdsville in 1957. It was located in the desert in 1986 during the Jubilee Mail Run re-enactment, and retrieved in 1993. A group of enthusiasts led by Neil Weidenbach, with the help of Tom, fully restored the Badger between 1996 and 1999. The truck was gifted by Tom and Valma to the people of Australia and is now on display in the National Motor Museum, at Birdwood in the Adelaide Hills. It is one of the featured vehicles in the National Motor Museum's installation *Sunburnt Country, Icons of Australian Motoring*.

Kruse retired in 1984 and moved to Cumberland Park in Adelaide. In the May 1986 South Australian 150th Jubilee, Tom re-enacted his run, with 80 vehicles joining in the northbound convoy. There was a second re-enactment in 1999, and in October of that year the Leyland was trucked to a few kilometres out of Birdsville so Tom could drive it into the township for celebrations. The next morning it was loaded with mail for 'The Mail Truck's Last Run' to Marree. A major reason for the event was to raise funds for the Royal Flying Doctor Service. This run resulted in another film documentary, *Last Mail from Birdsville – the Story of Tom Kruse*, as well as a book about Tom's life written by Kristin Weidenbach entitled *Mailman of the Birdsville Track*.

In 2000 Tom was inducted into the National Transport Hall of Fame in Alice Springs, and in 2003 he was officially recognised as an Outback Legend by *Australian Geographic* magazine. Also in 2003, Tom and his truck, the Badger, were nominated South Australian icons by the National Trust of Australia.

In 2008, bronze busts of Tom were placed in the National Transport Hall of Fame in Alice Springs, National Motor Museum at Birdwood, at Waterloo (his birthplace), and at Birdsville and Marree.

Publicans Phil and Marilyn (Maz) Turner of the iconic Marree Hotel commissioned Ian Doyle, Executive Producer of The Tom Kruse Collection to curate and, with Mark Metzger, to build the Tom Kruse Museum in the renamed Tom Kruse Room in the Marree Hotel. The collection includes hundreds of photographs, documents and memorabilia from Tom's Marree to Birdsville mail run, including a floor board and the original grille from the 1936 'Back of Beyond' Leyland Badger and a signed and framed mailbag used in the production of *Last Mail from Birdsville - the Story of Tom Kruse* in 1999. Kruse died in Adelaide, aged 96, on 30 June 2011.

MAX SCHUBERT 1915-1994

ORIGINATOR OF THE WORLD
FAMOUS GRANGE WINE

Max Schubert AM was a pioneering Australian winemaker, best known as the creator of Grange Hermitage. Schubert was included in a list of the 100 most influential Australians of the century, which was published in the *Sydney Morning Herald* in 2001.

Schubert was born to Lutheran parents in a German community on the fringes of the Barossa Valley, a region renowned for its winemaking. He joined Penfolds in 1931 as a messenger boy and became Penfolds first chief winemaker in 1948 at the age of 33, a position he held until 1975. Schubert spent his entire working life with Penfolds. He was described as:

A true company man, devoted to Penfolds. He was a humble and loyal servant of the Penfold family, and later of the public company.

Over the course of his career and beyond, Schubert received many awards, including Member of the Order of Australia (AM) and the inaugural Maurice O'Shea Award for his contribution to the Australian wine industry. He was also named 1988 Man of the Year by the UK's *Decanter Magazine*.

Schubert served in the Second World War, volunteering against the wishes of his Managing Director at Penfolds. He is believed to have saved the life of another Australia soldier when Stuka dive-bombers wiped out his convoy in north Africa, killing 200 men. He went on to serve in Greece, Crete, the Middle East, Ceylon and New Guinea, where he contracted malaria.

In 1949 Schubert was sent to France and Spain to learn more about fortified wine making, as fortified wines were the main production focus of Australian wineries during the period. As part of the trip he also visited the Bordeaux region, including first growth estates Château Lafite Rothschild, Château Latour and Château Margaux. Visiting these estates afforded him the opportunity to taste aged Bordeaux wines.

On his return to Australia, Schubert set about creating a wine for Penfolds that would similarly match the ability to age that he had seen in France. In 1951 the first experimental wine of the project was produced. Schubert named this wine Grange Hermitage, a combination of the name of the Penfold family cottage and the French appellation *Hermitage*. Unlike the Bordeaux wines, Grange was comprised not of Cabernet, but almost exclusively of Shiraz, the French appellation *Hermitage* applying to the Shiraz/Syrah growing area on the River Rhone.

Schubert stated that:

> *The method of production seemed fairly straightforward, but with several unorthodox features, and I felt that it would only be a matter of undertaking a complete survey of vineyards to find the correct varietal grape material. Then with a modified approach*

to take account of differing conditions, such as climate, soil, raw material and techniques generally, it would not be impossible to produce a wine which could stand on its own feet throughout the world and would be capable of improvement year by year for a minimum of 20 years.

1952 saw the first commercial release of Grange. Initially it did not receive a favourable reception. By 1957 Schubert was ordered by Penfolds management to cease production. However, Schubert still made the 1957, 1958 and 1959 vintages of Grange despite this direction.

A later tasting by the Penfolds Board of the early Grange wines met with much more favourable opinions, and a reprieve was granted for the production of Grange. The 1960 vintage enabled Schubert to return to using new oak barrels, something he had been unable to do during the 1957–59 vintages.

The 1955 vintage of Grange Hermitage was submitted to wine competitions, beginning in 1962, and over the years has won more than 50 gold medals. The 1971 vintage won first prize in Syrah/Shiraz at the Wine Olympics in Paris. The 1990 vintage was named Red Wine of the Year by *Wine Spectator* magazine in 1995, which later rated the 1998 vintage a 99 points out of a possible 100.

In 1962 Schubert created a wine that would become known as Bin 60A. Made from Cabernet Sauvignon from the Coonawarra (Sharam's Block and Block 20) and Barossa Valley shiraz (Kalimna Vineyard), the Bin 60A became Penfolds' most successful show wine, winning thirty-three gold medals and nineteen trophies in a short time span.

The experimental wine was produced in relatively small quantities, with a little over 400 cases of the wine produced. On release, the Bin 60A was acclaimed on the show circuit, and it received even greater acknowledgement after Max Schubert's death, when in 2004 *Decanter Magazine* named it as the only New World wine in its top 10 of the greatest wines of all time.

In 2008 respected Australian wine critic James Halliday said of the Bin 60A:

An utterly superb wine, a glorious freak of nature and man... The palate is virtually endless, with a peacock's tail stolen from the greatest of Burgundies... This is possibly the greatest red wine tasted in our times in Australia.

In 1953 Schubert created a solely Cabernet-based Grange, released with the moniker Bin 9. This wine was created using grapes from the Kalimna Block 42. Block 42 is said to be the site of the oldest continuously producing Cabernet Sauvignon vines on earth. In 1961 a Bin 58 Cabernet Sauvignon was produced using Block 42 fruit, and again in 1963 as Bin 63 – a wine that won the prestigious Jimmy Watson Memorial Trophy in 1964. In 1964 Schubert created the first Bin 707 wine from Block 42 fruit.

Schubert is also credited with the creation of Penfolds Bin series wine, beginning with Bin 28 in 1959, and followed by Bin 389 a year later in 1960.

His other innovations included the use of plastics, refrigeration, pH control, and cold stabilisation of white wines.

He received several awards, including Member of the Order of Australia (AM) and the inaugural Maurice O'Shea Award for his contribution to the Australian wine industry; and he was named 1988 Man of the Year by the British wine publication *Decanter*.

Schubert died in 1994, aged 79, at his home in Adelaide, South Australia. In his obituary the *New York Times* noted that his Grange had won more wine show prizes than any other Australian red wine, and was regarded as the flagship of Australia's wine industry.

In 1997 Max was posthumously honoured with the creation of the electoral district of Schubert in the South Australian House of Assembly, a seat in the lower house of the South Australian State Parliament. The electoral district includes the Barossa Valley wine region where Max Schubert was born and began working at Penfolds.

TOM ANGOVE 1918-2010

INVENTOR OF THE
CARDBOARD WINE CASK

The wine 'bag in a box' was patented in 1965 as an alternative to the half-gallon flagon. This may account for its nickname 'goon bag'. According to Tom Angove, it was inspired by the packaging of wine in goat skins in biblical times, but the 'airless bag' concept allowed the wine to remain fresh for six weeks after opening. In 1973 average wine consumption in Australia was 9.0L per year and in 1983 19.3L per year, largely due to the uptake of this new technology. The technology has now been taken up world-wide.

The Angoves are an innovative family. Dr William Angove arrived from Cornwall in 1886, set up practice at Tea Tree Gully and began producing wine (like Dr Lindeman and Dr Penfold). Thomas 'Skipper' Carlyon Angove (1880–1952) spent time at Cognac in France and returned to produce the famous double distilled St Agnes Brandy.

According to journalist Bob Byrne's account (The Advertiser, 2017), Tom Angove said: 'Glass breaks easily and then once opened, the wine is exposed to air and the quality deteriorates if it is not consumed fairly quickly, so why don't we put it in a plastic bag?' He wasn't the first to put liquid inside a plastic bag inside a rigid container, but he was the first to think that it could be a container for wine because of the airless flow principle. Tom's son John Angove said: 'The fundamental concept of airless flow is that when you take wine out of that flexible package there's no air going into it to replace the space that the wine was taking up. That fundamental concept is what's made it such a success.'

It took about two years to develop the bag in a box, and after some market research one gallon packs (about 4.5 litres) of table white, table red, port, sweet sherry and muscat were launched in November 1965.

'It continued to be a pretty strange idea,' said John. 'At the time there was nowhere you could go to buy a machine to fill the bag in the box. Dad had to develop how he was going to fill these things, how he was going to seal them and he hadn't gotten to the stage of the tapping device which, of course, is now standard for bag in a box.'

With the original casks the idea was to decant the wine through the top of the bag. You still had the airless flow and then you would reseal the top again with a paperclip or a peg. According to John the early product was a very rudimentary package.

It did take a long time for the reliability of the package to achieve a marketplace standard that the consumer was happy with. Initially there were many problems with trace leaks through the membrane and in pouring but over the years these improved, especially with a new tapping device in the late 1970s. Melbourne wine merchant Dan Murphy and Penfold's winemaker Ian Hickinbotham both worked on taps that would let wine out but stop air getting in. Penfold's first cask, in 1968, was a bag inside a round tin. Three years later, Wynns picked up on bag in a box technology which had been patented in the US for battery acid containers. Orlando took it to the next level with its highly successful marketing campaign: 'Where did you hide your Coolabah?'

In a 2002 interview for the National Wine Centre's History Project, Orlando's former operations manager, Perry Gunner, explains why the campaign worked:

It was often said about white wine, that (with) a cask of wine in the fridge, no one actually quite knew how much you were drinking. They even suggested that when Mum and Dad were away, the children would go and help themselves to the cask of Coolabah in the fridge.

Although the bag in a box has changed form over the years, the original concept that Tom Angove patented in 1965 has remained the same. Worldwide, a significant amount of wine drunk still comes from a cask. Whatever it has been called – goon bag, box wine, Balmain handbag or Chateau Cardboard – many Australians have fond memories of it. 'We've vacated that area many years ago,' says John Angove, 'but I'm sure Dad would be very proud to know that his little idea is now such an important part of today's global wine industry.'

DR BASIL HETZEL 1922-2017

CONQUEROR OF CRETINISM BY IODINE SUPPLEMENTATION

Dr Hetzel is known worldwide for his achievements in saving count-less thousands from cretinism (mainly in New Guinea and China) by supplementing salt with iodine, in which the diet was deficient. Basil was born in London to Elinor Hetzel (née Watt) and Kenneth Stuart Hetzel, an anaesthetist. His parents were originally from South Australia but were in London at the time while Kenneth worked at the University College Hospital. They returned to Adelaide in 1925. There, along with his brother Peter (born 1924), Basil was schooled at King's College and St Peter's College, Adelaide.

Hetzel studied medicine at the University of Adelaide from 1940 to 1944. As a medical student, he was granted reserved occupation status during World War II. He later applied to join the Royal Australian Air Force as a medical officer but was denied on grounds of being unfit due to a long bout of pulmonary tuberculosis in 1945.

In the 1950s he was a Fulbright Research Scholar, which included an appointment at New York Hospital. In 1954, Hetzel and his family travelled to London where he undertook a Research Fellowship in the Department of Endocrinology and Metabolism at St Thomas' Hospital.

His first job after completing medical studies was as a Resident Medical Officer at Parkside Mental Hospital from 1946 to 1947. Upon completion of his Fulbright Scholar commitments, Hetzel was appointed as the first Michell Research Scholar at the University of Adelaide, where he remained for three years. He then undertook the role of Reader in Medicine at the Queen Elizabeth Hospital, Adelaide, before moving to Monash University as the Foundation Professor of Social and Preventive Medicine. In 2001, the Queen Elizabeth Hospital established the Basil Hetzel Institute for Medical Research in his honour.

In 1956, Hetzel became a founding member of the South Australian Mental Health Association, and along with other members, went on to assist with the establishment of the crisis support service Lifeline, which still runs today.

He also held the position of first Chief of the CSIRO Division of Human Nutrition. Hetzel was the Chancellor of the University of South Australia from 1992, shortly after its establishment, until 1998. In 2005, the building for health sciences at the university's City East campus was named the Basil Hetzel building, and the campus library also has a Hetzel room which contains a collection of his research. Hetzel was Lieutenant Governor of South Australia from April 1992 to May 2000. He was Chair of the Bob Hawke Prime Ministerial Centre from 1998 to 2007.

Hetzel worked in remote areas of Papua New Guinea in the 1960s with the Public Health Department of the then Territory, and his research concluded that the endemic goitre and associated cretinism was attributable to an iodine-deficient diet. He also demonstrated that dietary supplementation would entirely prevent these illnesses. In his words, 'villages came alive'.

In the 1980s Hetzel, supported by the Australian Agency for International Development, became an international advocate for iodine supplementation, which is now taken for granted with iodinated table salt. This was part of the stimulus for the creation of the Iodine Global Network, then called the International Council for Control of Iodine Deficiency Disorders (ICCIDD), which is funded by various government, non-government and community organisations including the United Nations, the Global Alliance for Improved Nutrition, UNICEF, the World Health Organization, and the World Bank. The ICCIDD is considered the expert body regarding iodine deficiency disorders and they implement national programs for the prevention of iodine deficiency. As a result of their advocacy, many countries have now legislated that salt for human and animal consumption must be iodised. Much of this success has been attributed to Hetzel's 'indefatigable dedication to elimination of iodine deficiency disorders'. In 2010, the ICCIDD established a Basil Hetzel International Award for Communications for individuals who contribute to promoting awareness of iodine nutrition. It is claimed that iodine supplementation has been achieved in 70% of households worldwide by 2000.

Hetzel married Mary Helen Eyles in 1946. Together they had five children: Susan (born 1947), Richard (born 1949), Robert (born 1951), Jay (born 1952) and Elizabeth (born 1956). Helen died of cancer in December 1980. In 1983 Hetzel married again, to Anne Fisher.

Hetzel died on 4 February 2017, aged 94. His honours include: the Order of Australia; the Pollin Prize for Pediatric Research, 2009; the Prince Mahidol Award from King Bhumibol Adulyadej of Thailand; the National Trust National Living Treasure; Doctor of the University, University of South Australia; RSL Anzac Peace Prize; Companion of the Order of Australia; Honorary Professor at the Tianjin Medical University; the Susman Prize for Medical Research, Royal Australasian College of Physicians; and the Alwyn Smith Prize of the Faculty of Public Health Medicine, United Kingdom.

The Clinical Research Centre at the Queen Elizabeth Hospital was named The Basil Hetzel Institute for Medical Research in his honour.

DON DUNSTAN 1926-1999

INNOVATIVE SOUTH
AUSTRALIAN PREMIER

The Dunstan Decade was a great time to be in South Australia.

Don Dunstan was born in 1926. He became the Member for Norwood in 1953 and was Labor Premier in 1967/68 and 1970 to 1979. He was born in Suva but educated in Adelaide, studying Law and Arts at Adelaide University. He was a charismatic and aggressive debater. Dunstan campaigned against the death penalty whereupon the reigning Premier, Tom Playford, relented. After becoming Premier himself, Dunstan decriminalised homosexuality, improved Aboriginal rights, helped abolish the White Australia Policy, appointed the first female judge, the first non-British Governor, relaxed censorship and drinking laws, established a Ministry of the Environment, introduced anti-discrimination law, reformed the Legislative Council, reduced the voting age, instituted universal suffrage, gave support to the Adelaide Festival Centre and the State Theatre Company, and established the successful South Australian Film Corporation. He began cultural exchanges with Asia and improved culinary awareness. He resigned in 1979 after his wife died and a homosexual affair proved politically and personally unfortunate.

Dunstan's father was a shop manager for the Morris Hedstrom chain in Fiji. However, from an early age Don was educated in Australia, and grew up as part of the Adelaide establishment. In his youth, influenced by his uncle, former Liberal Lord Mayor of Adelaide Sir Jonathan Cain, Dunstan was a supporter of the conservative Liberal and Country League (LCL) and handed out how-to-vote cards for the party at state elections. Dunstan later said of his involvement with the Liberals: 'I do not call it snobbery to deride the Establishment in South Australia, I admit that I was brought up into it, and I admit that it gave me a pain.' When asked of his roots, he said: 'I'm a refugee from it and thank God for somewhere honest to flee to!'

He excelled academically before experiencing his progressive political awakening while training in law and arts at the University of Adelaide. He became very active in political organisations, joining the University Socialist Club, the Fabian Society, the Student Representative Council and the Theatre Group. A two-week stint in the Communist Party was followed by membership in the Australian Labor Party. Dunstan was markedly different from the general membership of the Labor Party of the time; when he applied for membership at Trades Hall, a Labor veteran supposedly muttered: 'How could that long-haired prick be a Labor man?' His peculiarities, such as his upper-class accent, were a target of derision by the working-class Labor old guard throughout his early political involvement. Dunstan funded his education by working in theatre and radio during his university years. He eventually graduated with a double degree, with arts majors in Latin, comparative philology, history and politics, and he came first in political science.

After Dunstan graduated he moved with his wife to Fiji, where he was admitted to the bar and began his career as a lawyer. They returned to Adelaide in 1951 and settled in George Street, Norwood, taking in boarders as a source of extra income.

Dunstan was nominated as the Labor candidate for the electoral district of Norwood at the 1953 election. His campaign was noted for his colourful methods for swaying voters: posters of his face were placed on every pole in the district, and Labor supporters walked the streets advocating Dunstan. He targeted in particular the large Italian migrant population of the district, distributing translated copies of a statement the sitting LCL member Roy Moir had made about immigrants. Moir had commented that 'these immigrants are of no use to us - a few of them are tradesmen but most of them have no skills at all. And when they intermarry we'll have all the colours of the rainbow'. Dunstan won the seat and was elected to the South Australian House of Assembly. His son Andrew was born nine months after the win.

Labor conducted an extensive campaign in marginal LCL seats at the 1965 election, resulting in 21 of 39 seats, with Frank Walsh and the Labor Party taking power. As Attorney-General and the number-two-man in the Government, the youthful and charismatic Dunstan made his older peers look lethargic as television became increasingly ubiquitous – television was new at the time and was also credited with the ascendance of John F Kennedy against Richard Nixon in 1960. The LCL opposition changed leaders and installed the young Steele Hall, which worried Labor as the elderly Walsh appeared bumbling in contrast. In response Labor replaced Walsh with Dunstan. Despite maintaining a much larger vote over the LCL, Labor lost two seats at the 1968 election, and the LCL formed a government with the support of an independent.

In the late 1950s, Dunstan became well known for his campaign against the death penalty being imposed on Max Stuart, who was convicted of the rape and murder of a small girl. He harried Playford aggressively over the matter, creating an uproar over what he saw as an unfair process. Playford eventually relented, and appeared shaken thereafter; the event was seen as a turning point in the LCL's popularity, and Labor gained momentum.

During Labor's time in opposition, Dunstan was prominent in securing some reforms in Aboriginal rights, and was at the forefront of Labor abandoning the White Australia Policy. Dunstan increased his attacks on the LCL gerrymander ('Playmander') and was able to convincingly sustain Playmander attacks with the effect of convincing the LCL into watering down the malapportionment. Again, with little change in Labor's vote but with the Playmander removed, Labor won 27 of 47 seats at the 1970 election. With a fairer seat and boundary system in place, Dunstan won three more elections, in 1973, 1975 and 1977.

A reformist, Dunstan brought profound change to South Australian society. His socially progressive administration saw Aboriginal land rights recognised, homosexuality decriminalised, the first female judge, the first non-British Governor, Sir Mark Oliphant, and later, the first indigenous Governor, Sir Douglas Nicholls. He enacted consumer protection laws, reformed and expanded the public education and health systems, abolished the death penalty, relaxed censorship and drinking laws, created a Ministry for the Environment, enacted anti-discrimination law; and he implemented electoral reforms such as the overhaul of the Legislative Council of Parliament, lowered the voting age to 18, enacted universal suffrage, and completely abolished malapportionment, changes which gave him a less hostile Parliament and allowed him to enact his reforms.

He established Rundle Mall in the place of Rundle Street, enacted measures to protect heritage buildings, and encouraged a flourishing of the arts, with support for the Adelaide Festival Centre, the State Theatre Company, and the establishment of the South Australian Film Corporation. He encouraged cultural exchanges with Asia, multiculturalism, and an increase in the state's culinary awareness and sophistication. He is recognised for his role in reinvigorating the social, artistic and cultural life of South Australia during his nine years in office, remembered as the Dunstan Decade.

However, there were also problems. The economy began to stagnate, and large increases to the burgeoning public service generated claims of waste. One of Dunstan's pet projects, a plan to build a new city at Monarto to alleviate urban pressures in Adelaide, was abandoned when economic and population growth stalled, with much money and planning already invested. After four consecutive election wins, Dunstan's administration began to falter in 1978 following his dismissal of Police Commissioner Harold Salisbury, as controversy broke out over whether he had improperly interfered with a judicial investigation. In addition, policy problems and unemployment began to mount, as well as unsubstantiated rumours of corruption and personal impropriety. Dunstan became increasingly short-tempered, and the strain was increased by the death of his second wife. His resignation from the premiership and politics in 1979 was abrupt after he collapsed due to ill health; but he lived for another 20 years, remaining a vocal and outspoken campaigner for progressive social policy.

Federally, together with fellow Australian Fabian Society member Gough Whitlam, Dunstan set about removing the White Australia policy from the Labor platform. The older trade-unionist-based members of the Labor Party vehemently opposed changing the status quo. However, the 'New Guard' of the party, of which Dunstan was a part, were determined to bring about its end. Attempts in 1959 and 1961 failed, with Labor leader Arthur Calwell stating: 'It would ruin the Party if we altered the immigration policy ... it was only cranks, long hairs, academics and do-gooders who wanted the change.' However, Dunstan persisted in his efforts, and in 1965 it was removed from the Labor platform at their national conference; Dunstan personally took credit for the change. Whitlam later brought about the comprehensive end of the White Australia policy in 1973 when he was Prime Minister.

Dunstan pursued similar reforms with respect to indigenous Australians. In 1962, the Aboriginal Affairs Bill was introduced to liberalise constraints that had been placed on indigenous Australians in the past and had effectively resulted in segregation. The initial proposal still retained some restrictions, placing more controls over full-blooded Aborigines. Dunstan was prominent in Labor's opposition to the double standards, and called for abolition of race-based restrictions, saying that social objectives could be achieved without explicit colour-based schemes. He was successful in forcing amendments to liberalise controls on property and the confinement of indigenous Australians to reserves. However, his attempt to remove the different standards required of part and full-blooded Aborigines failed, as did his proposal to ensure that at least half the members of the Aboriginal Affairs Board be indigenous Australians. Despite the passage of the Bill, restrictions remained in place and Dunstan questioned the policy of assimilation of Aborigines, which he saw as the diluting of their distinctive cultures.

Together with Mike Rann, his Press Secretary, speechwriter and eventually Premier, who had worked with him in 1978 on a series of speeches on Aboriginal Land Rights, industrial democracy and women's rights, Dunstan made a uranium fact-finding trip to Europe to study safe methods of nuclear power and waste disposal. The following summer, Dunstan fell extremely ill. When Parliament resumed, he collapsed on the floor of the House and was forced to use a walking stick; his doctor advised him that he required six months of rest to recover. The Liberal Opposition seized on the state of affairs and charged that the Labor Party was 'as ailing as the man who led it'. In a stage-managed press conference on 15 February 1979, Dunstan announced his retirement as Premier from his room in Calvary Hospital while shaking and wearing a dressing gown.

The political scientist Andrew Parkin said that one of Dunstan's main achievements was to debunk the notion that State Governments and Parliaments lacked the ability to make significant reforms with profound impacts. He cited Dunstan's sweeping social reforms and the fact that many other State Governments followed South Australia's lead as evidence of this.

From May 1980 to early 1981 Dunstan acted as editor for the magazine *POL*. In 1982, he moved to the neighbouring state of Victoria, and was appointed the Director of Tourism. This sparked an outcry in South Australia due to the two states' traditional rivalry. For his part, Dunstan said that he had yearned to be given a role in shaping and building the future of his native state, but that he had been snubbed for three years. He said that public figures in South Australia had told him that his high profile and ability to overshadow others could have caused a loss of face to them, and thus his departure would be seen favourably by them, while Victoria's offer gave him an opportunity to be constructive. Dunstan was appointed to the Victorian Economic Development Corporation on 12 July 1983 and resigned on 23 June 1986. Dunstan stayed in the Director of Tourism role until 1986, when he returned to Adelaide after falling out with the government of John Cain. His retirement from these positions followed the provocative publication of a photograph of him with Monsignor Porcamadonna, member of the gay community Order of Perpetual Indulgence, taken after he had launched a collection of coming out stories by gay historian Gary Wotherspoon.

He was the national President of the Freedom from Hunger Campaign (1982–87), President of the Movement for Democracy in Fiji (from 1987), and national Chairman of Community Aid Abroad (1992–93). Dunstan was an Adjunct Professor at the University of Adelaide from 1997 to 1999 and portrayed himself in the 1989 Australian independent film Against the Innocent.

In his retirement, Dunstan continued to be a passionate critic of economic rationalism (neoliberalism) and privatisation, particularly of South Australia's water, gas and electricity supplies. During the 1990s he wrote essays for the *Adelaide Review* magazine strongly criticising both the Federal Labor Governments of Bob Hawke and Paul Keating, the Federal Liberal Government of John Howard and the State Liberal Governments of Dean Brown and John Olsen. He remained an advocate for multiculturalism and cultural diversity, often writing about the dangers of racism. A year before his death, the ailing Dunstan decried Labor's economic rationalism in front of 5,000 at the Gough Whitlam Lecture. In his last interview, he decried economic rationalism as the 'nonsense of the Chicago school with which we've been beset'. Regardless of the acclaim in which he was held during his decade in power, Dunstan was largely overlooked for honours after leaving office and largely ignored by the state's elite. He was appointed a Companion of the Order of Australia in June 1979, but no national parks, gardens, buildings or performance venues were named after him.

Dunstan was afflicted by illness in his final years. He was diagnosed with throat cancer in 1993 then contracted an inoperable lung cancer, and died on 6 February 1999. A public memorial service was held on 9 February at the Adelaide Festival Centre as a tribute to Dunstan's love of the arts. In attendance were former Labor Prime Ministers Gough Whitlam and Bob Hawke, Federal Opposition Leader Kim Beazley, Premier John Olsen, and State Opposition Leader Mike Rann. Thousands more gathered outside the centre in Elder Park along the banks of the River Torrens. State flags were flown at half-mast and the memorial service was televised live.

Shortly before Dunstan's death, The Don Dunstan Foundation was established at the University of Adelaide to push for progressive change and to honour his memory. Dunstan had spent his last months helping to lay the platform for its establishment. At the inauguration of the body, he said: 'What we need is a concentration on the kind of agenda which I followed and I hope that my death will be useful in this.' The Foundation's primary work is the giving of scholarships; an additional aim is to promote causes championed by Dunstan such as human rights, social equality, multiculturalism and Aboriginal rights.

The Electoral Commission of South Australia's 2012 redistribution included renaming the seat of Norwood to Dunstan, as of the 2014 election. A biography entitled *Don Dunstan Intimacy & Liberty*, written by Dino Hodge with the co-operation of Dunstan's family and former lovers, was published in 2014.

In 1988 Dunstan donated a collection of files pertaining to his political, professional and personal life, photographs, press clippings, speeches and press releases, audiovisual material, books from his library, some items of clothing and other memorabilia to Flinders University Library, where it can be viewed and accessed for research.

Since its commencement in 2003, the Adelaide Film Festival has presented The Don Dunstan Award in recognition of outstanding contribution by an individual to the Australian film industry. Deemed by the Adelaide Film Festival's Board to have 'enriched Australian screen culture through their work', its recipients include David Gulpilil, Rolf de Heer, and Scott Hicks. After receiving the award in 2013, Hicks acknowledged Dunstan's vision for the creation of a film industry in South Australia as being instrumental to his professional development.

ROBIN WARREN 1937-

NOBEL PRIZE FOR MEDICINE

Who would have dreamed last century that peptic ulcers were caused by a bacterium? Robin Warren did and won the Nobel Prize for Medicine in 2005. A graduate of the University of Adelaide, Warren trained at the Royal Adelaide Hospital and became Registrar in Clinical Pathology at the Institute of Medical and Veterinary Science (now SA Pathology) where he worked in laboratory haematology. In 1963 he was Honorary Clinical Assistant in Pathology and Honorary Registrar in Haematology in the Royal Adelaide Hospital. He later became Clinical Pathology Registrar in the Royal Melbourne Hospital. He was awarded fellowship of the Royal College of Pathologists of Australasia in 1967 and then took up the post of Senior Pathologist at the Royal Perth Hospital, where he spent most of his career.

Robin Warren discovered a bacterium in the stomach lining of patients with peptic ulcers and named it *Helicobacter pylori (H Pylori)*. At the University of Western Australia he partnered with a gastroenterologist, Dr Barry Marshall, who was convinced by Robin that the organism caused stomach ulcers. An article in the prestigious medical journal *Lancet* stated:

> *In the world of medical research it would be hard to find two individuals working together whose temperaments were more diametrically opposed than Robin Warren and Barry Marshall, the joint winners of this year's Nobel Prize in Medicine. Warren, a consultant pathologist now retired from the Royal Perth Hospital in Australia, is a reserved man whose colleagues talk about his quiet persistence, thoughtfulness and careful observation. Marshall, a gastroenterologist, 14 years his junior from the University of Western Australia had described himself as brash. Others list his creativity, determination and entrepreneurial spirit.*

Together they proved that the bacterium actually caused the disease. Barry Marshall swallowed a culture of the organism in 1984, after which he started vomiting. Endoscopy (using a flexible telescope) showed that he had an inflamed stomach lining which was colonised by *H. pylori*. He took some antibiotics which had previously been shown to kill the bacterium and soon he was well again.

In the *Lancet* in 2005 Warren recalled: 'Every time I spoke to a clinician they would say "why hasn't it been described before?"' Orthodox medical teaching at the time was that bacteria did not grow in a normal stomach. Ten years later most specialists were still using major surgery to treat peptic ulcers, having dismissed Warren and Marshall's theory, but as more 'miracle' cures were reported, the antibiotic treatment gradually became mainstream. Warren developed a convenient diagnostic test (C14 urea breath test) for detecting the bacterium's presence in ulcer patients. He and Marshall won the Nobel Prize for Medicine in 2005.

In 2006 an Australian documentary, *The Winner's Guide to the Nobel Prize*, was made about Warren and Marshall's road to the Nobel Prize.

Robin Warren was appointed a Companion of the Order of Australia in 2007.

Asteroid 254863 Robinwarren, discovered by Italian amateur astronomer Silvano Casulli in 2005, was named in his honour. The official naming citation was published by the Minor Planet Center on 22 April 2016 (M.P.C. 99893).

J M COETZEE 1940-

NOBEL PRIZE FOR LITERATURE

John Maxwell Coetzee is a South African-born novelist, essayist, linguist, translator and recipient of the 2003 Nobel Prize in Literature. He relocated to Australia in 2002 and lives in Adelaide. He became an Australian citizen in 2006.

In 2013, Richard Poplak of the *Daily Maverick* described Coetzee as 'inarguably the most celebrated and decorated living English-language author'. Before receiving the 2003 Nobel Prize in Literature, Coetzee was awarded the Jerusalem Prize, CNA Prize (thrice), the *Prix Femina étranger*, *The Irish Times* International Fiction Prize and the Booker Prize (twice), among other accolades.

JM Coetzee was born in Cape Town, Cape Province, Union of South Africa, on 9 February 1940 to Afrikaner parents. His father, Zacharias Coetzee (1912–1988), was an occasional attorney and government employee, and his mother, Vera Coetzee (born Wehmeyer; 1904–1986), was a schoolteacher. The family mainly spoke English at home, but John spoke Afrikaans with other relatives. He is descended from early Dutch immigrants to South Africa in the 17th century on his father's side, while his mother was a descendant of Dutch, German and Polish immigrants.

Coetzee spent most of his early life in Cape Town and in Worcester in Cape Province (modern-day Western Cape), as recounted in his fictionalised memoir *Boyhood* (1997). The family moved to Worcester when he was eight, after his father had lost his government job. He attended St Joseph's College, a Catholic school in the Cape Town suburb of Rondebosch, later studying mathematics and English at the University of Cape Town and receiving his Bachelor of Arts with Honours in English in 1960 and his Bachelor of Arts with Honours in Mathematics in 1961.

He then relocated to the United Kingdom in 1962, worked as a computer programmer for IBM in London, and ICT (International Computers and Tabulators) in Bracknell and stayed until 1965. In 1963, while still in the UK, Coetzee was awarded a Master of Arts degree from the University of Cape Town for a thesis on the novels of Ford Madox Ford entitled *The Works of Ford Madox Ford with Particular Reference to the Novels* (1963). His experiences in England were later recounted in *Youth* (2002), his second volume of fictionalised memoirs.

In 1965 Coetzee went to the University of Texas at Austin, in the United States, on the Fulbright Program and received his doctorate in 1969. His PhD dissertation was a computer-aided stylistic analysis of Samuel Beckett's English prose. In 1968, he began teaching English literature at the State University of New York at Buffalo, where he stayed until 1971. In Buffalo he began his first novel, *Dusklands*.

From as early as 1968 he sought permanent residence in the United States, a process that was finally unsuccessful, in part due to his involvement in protests against the war in Vietnam. In March 1970, he had been one of 45 faculty members who occupied the university's Hayes Hall and were subsequently arrested for criminal trespass. The charges against the 45 were dropped in 1971. He then returned to South Africa to teach English literature at the University of Cape

Town, where he was promoted Professor of General Literature in 1983 and was Distinguished Professor of Literature between 1999 and 2001.

He retired in 2002 and relocated to Adelaide as an Honorary Research Fellow at the English Department of the University of Adelaide, where his partner, Dorothy Driver, is a fellow academic who had served as Professor on the Committee on Social Thought at the University of Chicago until 2003.

Coetzee has been the recipient of numerous awards throughout his career, although he has a reputation for avoiding award ceremonies.

He was the first writer to be awarded the Booker Prize twice: first for *Life & Times of Michael K* in 1983, and again for *Disgrace* in 1999. Two other authors also achieved this – Peter Carey (in 1988 and 2001) and Hilary Mantel (in 2009 and 2012).

Summertime, named on the 2009 longlist, was an early favourite to win an unprecedented third Booker Prize for Coetzee. It subsequently made the shortlist, but lost out to bookmakers' favourite and eventual winner *Wolf Hall* by Hilary Mantel. Coetzee was also longlisted in 2003 for *Elizabeth Costello* and in 2005 for *Slow Man*. *The Schooldays of Jesus*, a follow-up to his 2013 novel *The Childhood of Jesus*, was longlisted for the 2016 Booker Prize.

On 2 October 2003 Horace Engdahl, Head of the Swedish Academy, announced that Coetzee had been chosen as that year's recipient of the Nobel Prize in Literature, making him the fourth African writer to be so honoured and the second South African after Nadine Gordimer. When awarding the prize, the Swedish Academy stated that Coetzee 'in innumerable guises portrays the surprising involvement of the outsider'. The press release for the award also cited his 'well-crafted composition, pregnant dialogue and analytical brilliance', while focusing on the moral nature of his work. The prize ceremony was held in Stockholm on 10 December 2003.

He is a three-time winner of South Africa's CNA Prize. His *Waiting for the Barbarians* received both the James Tait Black Memorial Prize and the Geoffrey Faber Memorial Prize; *Age of Iron* was awarded the *Sunday Express* Book of the Year award, and *The Master of Petersburg* was awarded *The Irish Times* International Fiction Prize in 1995. He has also won the French *Prix Femina étranger*, the Commonwealth Writers' Prize, and the 1987 Jerusalem Prize for the Freedom of the Individual in Society.

Coetzee was awarded the Order of Mapungubwe (Gold Class) by the South African Government on 27 September 2005 for his 'exceptional contribution in the field of literature and for putting South Africa on the world stage'. He holds honorary doctorates from The American University of Paris, the University of Adelaide, La Trobe University, the University of Natal, the University of Oxford, Rhodes University, the State University of New York at Buffalo, the University of Strathclyde, the University of Technology, Sydney, the Adam Mickiewicz University in Poznań and the Universidad Iberoamericana.

In November 2014, Coetzee was honoured with a three-day academic conference entitled 'JM Coetzee in the World', held in his adopted city of Adelaide. It was described as 'the culmination of an enormous collaborative effort and the first event of its kind in Australia' and 'a reflection of the deep esteem in which John Coetzee is held by Australian academia'.

Coetzee is known to be reclusive and avoids publicity to such an extent that he did not collect either of his two Booker Prizes in person. The South African writer Rian Malan has said that:

Coetzee is a man of almost monkish self-discipline and dedication. He does not drink, smoke, or eat meat. He cycles vast distances to keep fit and spends at least an hour at his writing-desk each morning, seven days a week. A colleague who has worked with him for more than a decade claims to have seen him laugh just once. An acquaintance has attended several dinner parties where Coetzee has uttered not a single word.

Asked about this comment in an interview by email, Coetzee said, 'I have met Rian Malan only once in my life. He does not know me and is not qualified to talk about my character.'

As a result of his reclusive nature, signed copies of Coetzee's fiction are highly sought after. Recognising this, he was a key figure in the establishment of Oak Tree Press's *First Chapter Series*, limited edition signed works by literary greats to raise money for the child victims and orphans of the African HIV/AIDS crisis.

He married Philippa Jubber in 1963 and divorced in 1980. He has a son, Nicolas (born 1966) and a daughter, Gisela (born 1968) from this marriage. Nicolas died in 1989 at the age of 23 in an accident.

On 6 March 2006, Coetzee became an Australian citizen, and it has been argued that his 'acquired "Australianness" is deliberately adopted and stressed' (by Australians).

Along with André Brink and Breyten Breytenbach, Coetzee was, according to Fred Pfeil, at 'the forefront of the anti-apartheid movement within Afrikaner literature and letters'. In accepting the Jerusalem Prize in 1987, Coetzee spoke of the limitations of art in South African society, whose structures had resulted in 'deformed and stunted relations between human beings' and 'a deformed and stunted inner life'. He went on to say: 'South African literature is a literature in bondage. It is a less than fully human literature. It is exactly the kind of literature you would expect people to write from prison.' He called on the South African Government to abandon its apartheid policy. The scholar Isidore Diala states that JM Coetzee, Nadine Gordimer, and André Brink are 'three of South Africa's most distinguished white writers, all with definite anti-apartheid commitment'.

It has been argued that Coetzee's 1999 novel *Disgrace* allegorises South Africa's Truth and Reconciliation Commission (TRC). Asked about his views on the TRC, Coetzee stated, 'In a state with no official religion, the TRC was somewhat anomalous: a court of a certain kind based to a large degree on Christian teaching and on a strand of Christian teaching accepted in their hearts by only a tiny proportion of the citizenry. Only the future will tell what the TRC managed to achieve.' Following his Australian citizenship ceremony, Coetzee said:

*I did not so much leave South Africa, a country with which I retain
strong emotional ties, but come to Australia. I came because from
the time of my first visit in 1991, I was attracted by the free and
generous spirit of the people, by the beauty of the land itself and –
when I first saw Adelaide – by the grace of the city that I now have
the honour of calling my home.*

When he initially moved to Australia, he had cited the South African
government's lax attitude to crime in that country as a reason for the
move, leading to a spat with Thabo Mbeki, who, speaking of Coetzee's
novel *Disgrace* stated that 'South Africa is not only a place of rape'. In
1999, the African National Congress submission to an investigation into
racism in the media by the South African Human Rights Commission
named *Disgrace* as a novel depicting racist stereotypes. However, when
Coetzee won his Nobel Prize, Mbeki congratulated him 'on behalf of
the South African nation and indeed the continent of Africa'.

Coetzee has never specified any political orientation, although he
has alluded to politics in his work. Writing about his past in the third
person, Coetzee states in *Doubling the Point* that:

*Politically, the raznochinets can go either way. But during his
student years he, this person, this subject, my subject, steers clear of
the right. As a child in Worcester he has seen enough of the Afrikaner
right, enough of its rant, to last him a lifetime. In fact, even before
Worcester he has perhaps seen more of cruelty and violence than
should have been allowed to a child. So as a student he moves on
the fringes of the left without being part of the left. Sympathetic to
the human concerns of the left, he is alienated, when the crunch
comes, by its language – by all political language, in fact.*

Asked about the latter part of this quote in an interview, Coetzee
answered, 'There is no longer a left worth speaking of, and a language
of the left. The language of politics, with its new economistic bent, is
even more repellent than it was fifteen years ago.'

In February 2016, Coetzee was one of 61 signatories to a letter to Australian Prime Minister Malcolm Turnbull and Immigration Minister Peter Dutton, condemning their Government's policy of offshore detention of asylum seekers.

In 2005, Coetzee criticised contemporary anti-terrorism laws as resembling those employed by the apartheid regime in South Africa: 'I used to think that the people who created [South Africa's] laws that effectively suspended the rule of law were moral barbarians. Now I know they were just pioneers ahead of their time.' The main character in Coetzee's 2007 *Diary of a Bad Year*, which has been described as blending 'memoir with fiction, academic criticism with novelistic narration' and refusing 'to recognize the border that has traditionally separated political theory from fictional narrative', shares similar concerns about the policies of John Howard and George W Bush.

In recent years, Coetzee has become a vocal critic of animal cruelty and advocate for the animal rights movement. In a speech given on his behalf by Hugo Weaving in Sydney on 22 February 2007, Coetzee railed against the modern animal husbandry industry. The speech was for Voiceless, the animal protection institute, an Australian non-profit animal protection organisation, of which he became a patron in 2004. Coetzee's fiction has similarly engaged with the problems of animal cruelty and animal welfare, in particular his books *The Lives of Animals*, *Disgrace*, *Elizabeth Costello*, and *The Old Woman and the Cats*. He is a vegetarian.

In 2008, at the behest of John Banville, who alerted him to the matter, Coetzee wrote to *The Irish Times* of his agreement with Banville opposing Trinity College Dublin's use of vivisection on animals to conduct scientific research. Coetzee wrote:

I support the sentiments expressed by John Banville. There is no good reason — in fact there has never been any good reason, scientific or pedagogical - to require students to cut up living animals. Trinity College brings shame on itself by continuing with the practice.

Nearly nine years later, when Trinity College's continued (and, indeed, increasing) practice of vivisection featured in the news, a listener to the RTÉ Radio 1 weekday afternoon show *Liveline* pointed out that Banville had previously raised the matter but been ignored. Banville then personally telephoned *Liveline* to call the practice 'absolutely disgraceful' and recalled how his efforts to raise the matter and the intervention of Coetzee had been to no avail:

I was passing by the front gates of Trinity one day and there was a group of mostly young women protesting and I was interested. I went over and I spoke to them and they said that vivisection experiments were being carried out in the college. This was a great surprise to me and a great shock, so I wrote a letter of protest to The Irish Times. Some lady professor from Trinity wrote back essentially saying 'Mr. Banville should stick to his books and leave us scientists to our valuable work.' Asked if he received any other support for his stance in the letter he sent to The Irish Times, Banville replied: 'No... I became entirely dispirited and I thought, 'Just shut up, John. Stay out of it because I'm not going to do any good'. If I had done any good I would have kept it on. I mean, I got John Coetzee, you know, the famous novelist, J. M. Coetzee, I got him to write a letter to The Irish Times. I asked a lot of people.

Coetzee wanted to be a candidate in the 2014 European Parliament election for the Dutch Party for the Animals. However, his candidature was rejected by the Dutch election board, which argued that candidates had to prove legal residence in the European Union to be allowed.

For the period 2015–2018, Coetzee was a director of a seminar on the Literatures of the South at the Universidad Nacional de San Martín which involved writers and literary figures from Southern Africa, Australia and New Zealand, and South America. The aim of the seminars, one observer has remarked, is 'to develop comparative perspectives on the literature and journalism of the three areas in the southern hemisphere, to establish new intellectual networks, and to build a corpus of translated works from across the South through collaborative publishing ventures'. At the same time he has been involved in a research project in Australia, *Other Worlds: Forms of World Literature*, for which he is leading a theme on *Everyday Pleasures* that also is focused on the literatures of the South.

When asked to address unofficial Iranian translations of foreign works – Iran does not recognise international copyright agreements – Coetzee stated his disapproval of the practice on moral grounds and wished to have it sent to journalistic organisations in that country.

JAMES DIXON 'JIMMY' BARNES AO 1956–

SINGER, SONGWRITER

Jimmy Barnes was born on 28 April 1956. He is a Scottish-Australian rock singer and songwriter and his career as a solo performer and as the lead vocalist with the rock band Cold Chisel has made him one of the most popular and best-selling Australian music artists of all time. The combination of 14 Australian Top 40 albums for Cold Chisel and 13 charting solo albums, including nine Number Ones, gives Barnes the highest number of hit albums of any Australian artist.

James Swan (as Jimmy Barnes was known for the earliest years of his life) was born in Glasgow, Scotland. He arrived in Adelaide, South Australia as a five-year-old on 21 January 1962 with his parents Jim and Dorothy Swan and siblings John, Dorothy, Linda and Alan. Another sister, Lisa, was born in 1962, and the family eventually settled in Elizabeth, South Australia. His father, Jim Swan, was a prize fighter and his older brother John Swan, known as Swanee, also worked as a rock singer. John encouraged Jim and taught him how to sing as he was not initially interested. Shortly afterward, Barnes' parents divorced. His mother Dorothy soon remarried, to a clerk named Reg Barnes (died 3 September 2013).

Jimmy was raised a Protestant, and considers himself a Buddhist. In September 2009 he revealed that his maternal grandmother was Jewish.

Jimmy took an apprenticeship in a foundry with the South Australian Railways in 1973, but the love he and his brother had for music led him to join a band. Swanee was now playing drums with Fraternity, which had just parted ways with singer Bon Scott. Barnes took over the role but his tenure with the band was brief and before long he had joined a harder-edged band called Orange, featuring organist and songwriter Don Walker, guitarist Ian Moss, drummer Steve Prestwich and bassist Les Kaczmarek (who would be replaced by Phil Small within two years). Within a short time, the group had changed its name to Cold Chisel and began to develop a strong presence on the local music scene. Barnes' relationship with the band was often volatile and he left several times, leaving Moss to handle vocal duties until he returned. After a temporary move to Armidale, New South Wales, while Walker completed his engineering studies there, Cold Chisel moved to Melbourne in August 1976, and then three months later shifted base to Sydney. Progress was slow and Barnes announced he was leaving once again in May 1977 to join Swanee in a band called Feather. However, his farewell performance with Cold Chisel went so well that he changed his mind and decided to stay in the band, and a month later WEA signed the band.

By 1980 Cold Chisel was the biggest band in Australia and Barnes had developed a notorious reputation as a hard-drinking wild man who reportedly drank more than two bottles of vodka a day, much of it onstage during performances. While in Canberra in November 1979, he met Jane Mahoney (born 1958 as Jane Dejakasaya in Bangkok, Thailand), the stepdaughter of an Australian diplomat. Barnes began a relationship with her and they started living together, but in March 1980 she began to feel overwhelmed by the rock lifestyle and followed her family to Tokyo, where her father was posted. Barnes wrote the song 'Rising Sun' about this, and it appeared on the album *East*. The pair married in Sydney on 22 May 1981 and on 12 July 1982 Jane gave birth to their first child Mahalia, named after Mahalia Jackson. The couple have four children (Mahalia, Eliza-Jane, Elly-May and Jackie), who formed the group Tin Lids. Barnes had already fathered a son, singer David Campbell, who, due to the young age of his parents at the time of his birth (Barnes was 18 years old at the time), was being raised by his grandmother, but while Barnes maintained contact with him, Campbell did not become aware that Barnes was his father and not merely a family friend until the mid-1980s.

The singer had never been careful with money and the increasing pressure on him to provide for his young family caused even more tension between him and the rest of Cold Chisel. Despite being hugely successful in Australia, the group had still not been able to crack the market internationally. A disastrous tour of the United States in 1981 pulled them even further apart. While the 1982 album *Circus Animals* provided Cold Chisel with its second consecutive No.1 album, Barnes returned from the band's German tour in 1983 virtually broke. He asked for a $10,000 advance from the band's management but was refused, as the terms of the group's contract meant that if one member was given such a sum, the rest of them were entitled to the same amount. At a meeting in August, it was decided that Cold Chisel should split up. The group had already begun to fragment – Ray Arnott had replaced Steve Prestwich earlier in the year. Sessions for the final album were spread across different studios as various members refused to work together, but at the end of the year *The Last Stand* farewell tour (with Prestwich back in the band) became the highest-grossing concert-series by an Australian band ever. The group gave its final performance in Sydney on 12 December 1983, reportedly precisely ten years after its original formation. The film of that show remains the best-selling live-concert film of any Australian band.

Barnes had recorded seven albums with Cold Chisel between 1978 and 1983, including two live albums (the second of which,

Barking Spiders Live 1983, was released in 1984). He was arguably now Australia's highest-profile rock singer.

Barnes launched his own career less than a month after Cold Chisel's Last Stand tour came to an end. He assembled a band that included Arnott, former Fraternity bass player Bruce Howe and guitarists Mal Eastick (ex-Stars) and Chris Stockley (ex-The Dingoes) and began touring and writing for a solo album. Signing to Mushroom Records, Barnes released his first solo album *Bodyswerve*. He was now billing himself as Jimmy Barnes instead of Jim Barnes, as he had been credited during his Cold Chisel days. The album was immediately successful, entering the Australian charts at Number One on 8 October. This was the first of a remarkable run of top charting albums for Barnes, as each of his first six solo albums all debuted in the Number One position, a feat that no other Australian musical artist is likely to match. His list of Number One albums now totals eleven, including three Cold Chisel albums. His total of nine Number One albums as a solo performer is matched by no other Australian recording artist. The final Cold Chisel studio album *20th Century* and the live album *Barking Spiders Live* were also released in 1984. *20th Century* peaked at No.1 on 23 April.

On 22 December 1984, days after Barnes had begun that year's *Barnestorming* tour, his second daughter, Eliza-Jane ('E.J.'), was born. Early in his solo career, Barnes was determined to break into the US market and signed to Geffen Records for release there. His second album *For the Working Class Man* was tailored in this direction, featuring remixed songs from *Bodyswerve* plus five new tracks including 'Working Class Man' that was written by Journey musician Jonathan Cain and would become Barnes' signature tune. Several US musicians worked on the album including Cain, Charlie Sexton, singer Kim Carnes and British drummer Mick Fleetwood of Fleetwood Mac. The album was released as a double vinyl set and sold 250,000 copies in twelve months in Australia. Like its predecessor, *For the Working Class Man* debuted on the national chart at No.1 on 16 December 1985. It remained at No.1 for seven weeks. Titled simply *Jimmy Barnes* in the US, the album was issued in February to tie in with the release of the Ron Howard film

Gung Ho which featured 'Working Class Man'. Because of this, the film *Gung Ho* was released as *Working Class Man* in Australia.

The Jimmy Barnes band that toured Australia in support of the album featured Howe and Arnott, plus keyboardist Peter Kekell, former Rose Tattoo guitarist Robin Riley and American guitarist Dave Amato. With the release of the album in America, Barnes headed off with a band of Canadian musicians hand-picked by his North American management team and toured with ZZ Top. It was the first time since 1981 that he had toured without his family as part of his entourage, as Jane was pregnant. Shortly after their son Jackie (named after Jackie Wilson) was born on 4 February 1986, she and the children joined him in the US for the rest of the tour. In 1986, Barnes recorded two songs with INXS, an Easybeats cover, 'Good Times,' and 'Laying Down The Law', which he co-wrote with INXS members Andrew Farriss and Michael Hutchence. 'Good Times' was used as the theme song for the Australian Made series of concerts that toured the country in the summer of 1986–87. At the time, Australian Made was the largest touring festival of Australian music talent that had ever been attempted. Barnes and INXS headlined and the rest of the line-up featured Mental as Anything, Divinyls, Models, The Saints, I'm Talking and The Triffids. The shows began in Hobart, Tasmania on 26 December and concluded in Sydney on Australia Day, 26 January 1987. A concert film of this event was made by Richard Lowenstein and released later that year. 'Good Times' peaked at No.2 on the Australian chart and several months later was featured in the Joel Schumacher film *The Lost Boys*, allowing it to chart in the Top 40 in the US.

'The Good Times'/'Laying Down the Law' release was the first in a long line of songs Barnes recorded with other well-known singers and artists. In 1991 he recorded a version of 'When Something is Wrong with My Baby' with John Farnham as a single and centrepiece track for his *Soul Deep* album. The following year he released a version of 'Simply The Best' as a duet with Tina Turner that was used as the theme song for that year's Australian Rugby League advertising campaign. It peaked at No.13 in Australia. His 1993 album *Flesh and Wood* also featured several duets, including songs with Joe Cocker, Archie Roach, Tommy Emmanuel and a version of The Band's 'The Weight' with The Badloves.

The next album release, *Freight Train Heart* (1987), again featured contributions from a range of US musicians including Huey Lewis, Journey members Randy Jackson and Neal Schon and former Babys and Rod Stewart drummer Tony Brock, who later accompanied Barnes on tour. The recording process was deeply problematic, however, as Barnes fought with producer Jonathan Cain over artistic control and Geffen Records wanted to feature a solo by Robert Cray in the track 'Too Much Ain't Enough Love' in place of the one laid down by Schon. In the end, Barnes claimed the masters and returned to Sydney to rework the recording with English producer Mike Stone. Most of the songs were remixed, with parts added by Peter Kekell, Rick Brewster from The Angels, and Johnny Diesel, the 20-year-old guitarist and frontman of Perth band Johnny Diesel and the Injectors, who had just begun to make a name for themselves. Jon Farriss from INXS and ex-Angels bassist Chris Bailey also played on the album. Diesel, Kekell, Brock, Bailey and Dave Amato were kept on as Barnes' touring band, which hit the road in November just ahead of the release of the first single, 'Too Much Ain't Enough Love', in December 1987. It became Barnes' first No.1 hit single. The album followed the trend set by the previous two, and it debuted in the No.1 slot on 21 December. *Freight Train Heart* found moderate success outside Australia, and in 2003 it was named as one of the top 100 rock albums of all time by British magazine *Powerplay*. His problems with Geffen during the recording process caused him to sever his relations with them and he eventually signed to Atlantic in 1990.

In Australia, Barnes' success remained virtually unmatched. The Number One success of his first three albums continued with the live album *Barnestorming*, recorded during the promotional tour of the same name, which peaked at No.1 for three weeks from 5 December. A version of the Percy Sledge standard 'When A Man Loves A Woman' lifted from the album was a No.3 hit. His next tour brought controversy by being underwritten by Pepsi, which allowed him to expand the production and increase promotion, and at the end of the tour he made a $25,000 donation to the Children's Hospital in Camperdown, Sydney. In the middle of 1989, Jane Barnes went into Westmead Children's Hospital in Sydney with pregnancy complications; Elly-May Barnes was born almost three months prematurely on 3 May. Her father held off all further writing and recording until she was released from a humidicrib several months later.

Barnes signed to Atlantic for worldwide release in mid-1990 and immediately headed into the studio with producer Don Gehman to record *Two Fires*. The album featured songwriting contributions from the likes of Desmond Child, Diane Warren and Holly Knight, whose track became the title of his record and vocal contributions from Brian Setzer, and from his wife and children. Collectively known as The Tin Lids (after Glaswegian rhyming-slang for 'kids'), the four Barnes children later recorded three albums of their own. *Two Fires* combined live drums with synthesised drum machines and contained the hits 'Lay Down Your Guns', 'Make it Last All Night', 'When Your Love is Gone' and 'Little Darling'. It had a slight funk influence and an even more polished sound than his previous albums but this proved no barrier to it becoming his fifth consecutive Australian No.1 album.

The following year he released *Soul Deep*, an album of soul covers. Barnes had long fostered a love for soul and black music, naming his children after influential black artists and including songs by Sam Cooke and Percy Sledge on previous albums. He and Gehman had discussed the idea during the sessions for *Two Fires* and both had apparently decided that it would be 'a fun thing to do'. *Soul Deep* went on to become Jimmy Barnes' most successful album ever, spawning the No.3 single 'When Something is Wrong with My Baby', a duet with John Farnham. Re-releases of the album were issued in special gate-fold sleeves with embossed gold lettering, collector cards and extra live tracks.

The 1993 album *Heat* saw Barnes return to hard rock. Influenced by the then-current grunge trend and the music of the Red Hot Chili

Peppers, *Heat* was an attempt to move back to Barnes' raw rock 'n' roll roots after the polished sound of *Soul Deep* and *Two Fires*. While described as his most interesting album, it broke his run of Number One releases (it peaked at No.2) but did contain the hit 'Stone Cold', written by former Cold Chisel bandmate Don Walker. It was the first time Jimmy Barnes had worked with any member of his old band for almost a decade. The pair teamed up for an acoustic version of the track for an unplugged album *Flesh and Wood*, which appeared later the same year. *Flesh and Wood* reached No.1 on the Australian album chart. It included a version of The Band's 'The Weight', recorded with The Badloves, which became a hit. Also in 1993, Barnes teamed up with Tina Turner for a duet version of 'The Best' in the form of a TV promotion for rugby league's Winfield Cup. The single reached the top ten that year.

Following this, in the mid-1990s, Jimmy Barnes' career suffered a slump. The singer faced financial ruin as his music publishing company Dirty Sheet Music and his wife's children's fashion label both went broke. He was pursued by both the ANZ Bank and the Australian Taxation Office for amounts exceeding $1.3 million. The family sold their property in Bowral, New South Wales, and settled for some time in Aix-en-Provence, France, attracting some adverse publicity when Barnes assaulted a television crew from Channel 7. While there, he did considerable live work throughout Britain and toured with the Rolling Stones. His 1995 album *Psyclone* reached Number 2 in Australia and featured the top ten hit 'Change of Heart', but it did not sell as well as previous albums. In 1996 the greatest hits compilation *Barnes Hits Anthology* returned Jimmy Barnes to the top of Australian charts, along with the hit single 'Lover Lover' which was written by his wife. It was the beginning of a comeback that was hastened by the re-formation of Cold Chisel in 1998, coinciding with his return to Australia with his family after three years in France.

In March 1999 he performed the 1978 Sylvester hit 'You Make Me Feel (Mighty Real)' live onstage at the Sydney Gay and Lesbian Mardi Gras' annual party.

Later that year Barnes released the heavy rock single 'Love and Hate', followed by its parent album *Love and Fear*. An autobiographical record combining hard rock with electronic music, *Love and Fear* was Barnes' first album to miss the Australian top ten.

The comeback was continued with another string of solo releases, including a second album of soul tunes, *Soul Deeper... Songs From the Deep South* (ARIA No. 3, 2000), and two live albums, the first an acoustic performance and the second a performance of his soul songs. He appeared live on stage with INXS at some shows throughout Australia between 1999 and 2001, but the reception to this was not encouraging. He also performed at the closing ceremony of the Sydney Olympics in 2000.

In 2004, Barnes recorded an album with Deep Purple guitarist Steve Morse, Uriah Heep drummer Lee Kerslake, bass player Bob Daisley and keyboard player Don Airey under the name Living Loud. The self-titled album featured a number of songs originally written and recorded with Ozzy Osbourne by Kerslake, Daisley and Airey. *Double Happiness*, released in July 2005, reaffirmed his popularity, debuting at No.1 on the ARIAnet Albums Chart, his seventh album to do so. *Double Happiness* was a complete album of duets, including several with his children, daughters Mahalia and Elly-May, son Jackie and oldest son, entertainer David Campbell. Roachford, Smoky Dawson, Ian Moss and Tim Rogers of You Am I are among others who appear. After its initial success, it was re-released as a double CD/DVD package featuring many of his duets from previous albums, including those with INXS, John Farnham, Joe Cocker and Tina Turner. *Double Happiness* was followed in 2006 by a karaoke DVD version that featured many of his songs minus the vocal track.

Barnes was inducted into the ARIA Hall of Fame on 23 October 2005 for his solo career efforts, and coupled with Cold Chisel's 1993 induction, Barnes has entered into the Hall of Fame twice. In late 2006, Barnes became patron of the Choir of Hard Knocks, a choral group formed by Jonathon Welch and consisting of homeless and disadvantaged people in Melbourne. The formation of the choir was documented by the ABC as a five-part series aired in May 2007. Despite his health problems, Barnes took an active part in teaching the choir and has even busked with them. Barnes or a member of his extended family have regularly performed 'Flame Trees' with the Choir at their concerts including those at Melbourne Town Hall on 24 June and the Sydney Opera House on 17 July 2007. He underwent heart surgery in February 2007 and then in May, the boxed CD set *50* was released, featuring remastered versions of all his studio albums and a double CD of rare tracks. The collection was limited to 5000 copies. On 7 July 2007 Barnes was a presenter at the Australian leg of Live Earth. In August he became a regular presenter on *The Know*, a pop culture program on the pay TV channel MAX and has also been a presenter of the *Planet Rock* program on the Austereo network.

In September 2007 he started recording his 13th studio album, *Out in the Blue*. Produced by Nash Chambers, it was released on 14 November and debuted in the ARIA chart at No.3. The songs were written while he recovered from his heart surgery, and he displayed a more subdued mood than much of his previous output. 'When Two Hearts Collide' was a duet with Kasey Chambers. The album was promoted with a performance at the Sydney Opera House, which was released on CD and DVD.

Jimmy Barnes continues to recognise and give support to young bands and artists in Australia. In a January 2007 interview with *The Bulletin*, he spoke passionately about Australian rock musicians saying: 'Australian bands for me will always have the grunt. Grunt is what gives you longevity, strength, the power to believe in yourself. We have great bands here because they play live, they cut their teeth playing to people.' In March 2008, Barnes appeared as a special guest during soul singer Guy Sebastian's tour.

In September 2008 he undertook a tour of Europe. In November he released a duet with son David Campbell, a cover of The Righteous Brothers' 'You've Lost That Lovin' Feeling' that featured on Campbell's album *Good Lovin*. In September the following year his fifteenth studio album *The Rhythm and the Blues* was released, immediately becoming his ninth No.1 solo release, and giving him more No.1 albums than any other Australian artist. The same week, after hinting about the possibility during his appearance on *Good News Week*, it was announced that Cold Chisel would play at the V8 Supercars race in Sydney on 5 December 2009.

Also in 2008, Barnes became the face of the Intensive Care Appeal, a major fund-raising event held annually in Australia and New Zealand for the Intensive Care Foundation. The goal of the Appeal is to create awareness and raise funds for critically ill patients in intensive-care units.

Barnes released *Rage and Ruin* on 27 August 2010, his first album of original material since 2007. He has stated that the ideas for most of the lyrics and song themes came from a journal he kept during a period in his life (late 1990s to early 2000s) when he struggled with drug and alcohol addiction. Two singles have been released from the album: 'Before the Devil Knows You're Dead' and 'God or Money'. The album debuted at Number 3 on the ARIA Albums Chart on 5 September 2010. Three weeks later, on 27 September, it was revealed that Barnes has two adult daughters he had never previously met.

On 14 March 2011 he planted a flame tree, made famous in Cold Chisel's 1984 song 'Flame Trees', at the National Arboretum Canberra. He then headlined at Celebrate in the Park, playing a 90-minute set which included his solo hits and some Cold Chisel greats. He was joined by daughter Mahalia in a soulful rendition of 'When the War Is Over', which he dedicated to the memory of Steve Prestwich.

In August 2014, Barnes released a new album, titled *30:30 Hindsight*, which is an anniversary album, celebrating 30 years since his chart-topping debut solo album, *Bodyswerve*. It debuted at No.1 in Australia. This was Barnes' 10th solo No.1 album.

In 2015, Barnes asked the Reclaim Australia Political Party to stop playing his music at their Rallies. In July 2015, it was announced that Barnes would release *Best of the Soul Years* compilation. The album would be compiled of soul and R&B classics, from his three soul albums, *Soul Deep* (1991), *Soul Deeper* (2000) and *The Rhythm and the Blues*

(2009). Two new tracks were included on the album, Wilson Pickett classics, 'In the Midnight Hour' and 'Mustang Sally'. The album was released on 14 August 2015. A new album of soul covers was released in June 2016 called, *Soul Searchin'*. Jimmy Barnes also mentored and contributed to Reece Mastin's *Change Colours* album.

In 2016, Barnes released his autobiography, *Working Class Boy*, which explored his traumatic childhood experiences. In 2017, he featured in the song 'Big Enough' by Kirin J Callinan, alongside Alex Cameron and Molly Lewis. The song was featured on *The Tonight Show with Jimmy Fallon* in a comedic skit. In addition to this, his cameo in the song's music video became a popular internet meme in late 2017. In March of the same year, Barnes released a children's album called *Och Aye the G'nu*. It won the ARIA Award for Best Children's Album at the ARIA Music Awards of 2017, although the brand that appeared on the album, as well as the poetry books that were released on the first of April are related to The Wiggles.

In November 2017, Barnes released a second memoir, a sequel to *Working Class Boy* titled *Working Class Man*. On 3 May 2018, Barnes won the Biography of the Year award at the Australian Book Industry Awards for the second year in a row.

Barnes also guest starred in the television comedy *These New South Whales* based on the Australian band.

His autobiography *Working Class Boy* was adapted into a film by Universal Pictures. Directed by Mark Joffe, the film premiered in Australian cinemas on 23 August 2018. A soundtrack was released on 17 August 2018.

In January 2019, Barnes announced his 17th solo studio album *My Criminal Record* would be released on 17 May 2019.

STUDIO ALBUMS
- *Bodyswerve* (1984)
- *For the Working Class Man* (1985)
- *Freight Train Heart* (1987)
- *Two Fires* (1990)

- *Soul Deep* (1991)
- *Heat* (1993)
- *Flesh and Wood* (1993)
- *Psyclone* (1995)
- *Love and Fear* (1999)
- *Soul Deeper... Songs From the Deep South* (2000)
- *Double Happiness* (2005)
- *Out in the Blue* (2007)
- *The Rhythm and the Blues* (2009)
- *Rage And Ruin* (2010)
- *30:30 Hindsight* (2014)
- *Soul Searchin'* (2016)
- *Och Aye the G'nu* (2017)
- *Working Class Boy (soundtrack)* (2018)
- *My Criminal Record* (2019)

In 2017 Barnes was appointed an Officer of the Order of Australia for distinguished service to the performing arts as a musician, singer and songwriter, and through support for not-for-profit organisations, particularly to children with a disability.

Barnes has won six Australian Recording Industry Association (ARIA) Awards, including his induction into their Hall of Fame in 2005.

TERENCE TAO 1975-

WINNER OF FIELDS MEDAL
FOR MATHEMATICS

Terry Tao, born in Adelaide, exhibited extraordinary mathematical abilities from an early age, attending university level mathematics courses at the age of nine. He and Lenhard Ng are the only two children in the history of the Johns Hopkins' Study of Exceptional Talent program to have achieved a score of 700 or greater on the SAT math section while just nine years old; Tao scored 760. Tao was the youngest participant to date in the International Mathematical Olympiad, first competing at the age of ten; in 1986, 1987, and 1988, he won a bronze, silver, and gold medal. He remains the youngest winner of each of the three medals in the Olympiad's history, winning the gold medal shortly after his thirteenth birthday. In 2006 he won the Fields Medal, the greatest international prize in mathematics.

Tao's father, Dr Billy Tao, is an Adelaide pediatrician who was born in Shanghai, China, and earned his medical degree from the University of Hong Kong in 1969. Tao's mother Grace is from Hong Kong; she received a first class honours degree in physics and mathematics at the University of Hong Kong. She was a secondary school teacher of mathematics and physics in Hong Kong. Billy and Grace met as students at the University of Hong Kong, and then emigrated to South Australia.

Tao has two brothers, Nigel and Trevor, living in Australia. Both formerly represented Australia at the International Mathematical Olympiad.

Tao's wife, Laura, is an engineer at NASA's Jet Propulsion Laboratory. They live with their son and daughter in Los Angeles, California.

The story is told that when he was four years old, Terry was visited by a university maths lecturer to test his acumen. She couldn't properly assess his ability at long division because she had not brought her calculator! At 14, Tao attended the Research Science Institute. When he was 15, he published his first assistant paper. In 1991, he received his Bachelor's and Master's degrees at the age of 16 from Flinders University under Garth Gaudry. In 1992, he won a Postgraduate Fulbright Scholarship to undertake research in Mathematics (Topology) at Princeton University in the United States. From 1992 to 1996, Tao was a graduate student at Princeton University under the direction of Elias Stein, receiving his PhD at the age of 21. Then, in 1996, he joined the faculty of the University of California, Los Angeles. In 1999, when he was 24, he was promoted to full Professor at UCLA and remains the youngest person ever appointed to that rank by the institution.

Within the field of mathematics, Tao is known for his collaboration with Ben J Green of Oxford University; together they proved the Green-Tao theorem. Known for his collaborative mindset, by 2006, Tao had worked with over 30 others in his discoveries, reaching 68 co-authors by October 2015.

In a book review, the mathematician Timothy Gowers remarked on Tao's accomplishments:

Tao's mathematical knowledge has an extraordinary combination of breadth and depth: he can write confidently and authoritatively on topics as diverse as partial differential equations, analytic number theory, the geometry of 3-manifolds, nonstandard analysis, group theory, model theory, quantum mechanics, probability, ergodic theory, combinatorics, harmonic analysis, image processing, functional analysis, and many others. Some of these are areas to which he has made fundamental contributions. Others are areas that he appears to understand at the deep intuitive level of an expert despite officially not working in those areas. How he does all this, as well as writing papers and books at a prodigious rate, is a complete mystery. It has been said that David Hilbert was the last person to know all of mathematics, but it is not easy to find gaps in Tao's knowledge, and if you do then you may well find that the gaps have been filled a year later.

Tao has won numerous honours and awards over the years.

He is a Fellow of the Royal Society, the Australian Academy of Science (Corresponding Member), the National Academy of Sciences (Foreign Member), the American Academy of Arts and Sciences, and the American Mathematical Society. In 2006 he received the prestigious Fields Medal 'for his contributions to partial differential equations, combinatorics, harmonic analysis and additive number theory', and was also awarded the MacArthur Fellowship. He has been featured in *The New York Times*, CNN, *USA Today*, *Popular Science*, and many other media outlets.

By 2016, Tao had published about 300 research papers and 17 books. He has an Erdős number of 2. In 2018, Tao proved Bounding the de Bruijn-Newman constant.

In 2004, Ben Green and Tao released a preprint proving what is now known as the Green-Tao theorem. This theorem states that there are arbitrarily long arithmetic progressions of prime numbers. *The New York Times* described it this way:

> *In 2004, Dr. Tao, along with Ben Green, a mathematician now at the University of Cambridge in England, solved a problem related to the Twin Prime Conjecture by looking at prime number progressions— series of numbers equally spaced. (For example, 3, 7 and 11 constitute a progression of prime numbers with a spacing of 4; the next number in the sequence, 15, is not prime.) Dr. Tao and Dr. Green proved that it is always possible to find, somewhere in the infinity of integers, a progression of prime numbers of equal spacing and any length.*

For this and other work Tao was awarded the Australian Mathematical Society Medal of 2004. He was awarded a Fields Medal in August 2006 at the 25th International Congress of Mathematicians in Madrid. He was the first Australian, the first UCLA faculty member, and one of the youngest mathematicians to receive the award.

An article by *New Scientist* writes of his ability:

> *Such is Tao's reputation that mathematicians now compete to interest him in their problems, and he is becoming a kind of Mr Fix-it for frustrated researchers. 'If you're stuck on a problem, then one way out is to interest Terence Tao,' says Charles Fefferman [professor of mathematics at Princeton University].*

Tao was a finalist to become Australian of the Year in 2007. He is a Corresponding Member of the Australian Academy of Science, and in 2007 was elected as a Fellow of the Royal Society. In the same year Tao also published *Tao's inequality, an extension to the Szemerédi regularity lemma* in the field of information theory.

In April 2008, Tao received the Alan T Waterman Award, which recognises an early career scientist for outstanding contributions in their field. In addition to a medal, Waterman awardees also receive a $500,000 grant for advanced research.

In December 2008, he was named the Lars Onsager lecturer of 2008, for 'his combination of mathematical depth, width and volume in a manner unprecedented in contemporary mathematics'. He was presented with the Onsager Medal, and held his Lars Onsager lecture entitled *Structure and randomness in the prime numbers* at Norges Teknisk-Naturvitenskaplige Universitet (NTNU), Norway.

Tao was also elected a Fellow of the American Academy of Arts and Sciences in 2009.

In 2010, he received the King Faisal International Prize jointly with Enrico Bombieri. Also in 2010, he was awarded the Nemmers Prize in Mathematics and the Polya Prize (SIAM) jointly with Emmanuel Candès for their work on Compressed Sensing.

In 2007, Tao and Van H Vu solved the circular law conjecture.

In 2010, joint work with Ben Green culminated in the proof of the Hardy-Littlewood prime tuples conjecture for any linear system of finite complexity.

Tao also made contributions to the study of the Erdős-Straus conjecture in 2011, by showing that the number of solutions to the Erdős-Straus equation increases polylogarithmically as n tends to infinity.

In 2012, he and Jean Bourgain received the Crafoord Prize in Mathematics from the Royal Swedish Academy of Sciences. Also, in 2012, he was selected as a Simons Investigator. He proved that every odd integer greater than 1 is the sum of at most five primes.

In 2012, in joint work with longtime co-author Ben Green, proofs were announced for the Dirac-Motzkin conjecture and the 'orchard-planting problem' (which asks for the maximum number of lines through exactly 3 points in a set of n points in the plane, not all on a line). That same year, Tao published the first monograph on the topic of Higher Order Fourier Analysis.

In 2014, Tao received a CTY Distinguished Alumni Honor from Johns Hopkins Center for Gifted and Talented Youth in front of 963 attendees in 8th and 9th grade that are in the same program that Tao graduated from. That year, Tao presented work on a possible attack on the notorious Navier–Stokes existence and smoothness Millennium Problem, by establishing finite time blowup for an averaged three-dimensional Navier-Stokes equation. That year he also, jointly with several co-authors, proved several results on short and long prime gaps.

In September 2015, Tao announced a proof of the Erdős discrepancy problem, using for the first time entropy-estimates within analytic number theory.

Tao received the Salem Prize in 2000, the Bôcher Memorial Prize in 2002, and the Clay Research Award in 2003, for his contributions to analysis including work on the Kakeya conjecture and wave maps. In 2005, he received the American Mathematical Society's Levi L Conant Prize with Allen Knutson for a proof of the Horn conjecture, and in 2006 he was awarded the SASTRA Ramanujan Prize. The following is a summary of these awards:

- Fulbright Scholarship (1992)
- Salem Prize (2000)
- Bôcher Memorial Prize (2002)
- Clay Research Award (2003)
- Australian Mathematical Society Medal (2005)
- Ostrowski Prize (2005)
- Levi L Conant Prize (2005)
- ISAAC award (2005)
- Fields Medal (2006)
- MacArthur Award (2006)
- SASTRA Ramanujan Prize (2006)
- Sloan Fellowship (2006)
- Fellow of the Royal Society (2007)
- Alan T Waterman Award (2008)
- Convocation Award (2008)
- Onsager Medal (2008)
- Inducted into the American Academy of Arts and Sciences (2009)
- King Faisal International Prize (2010)
- Nemmers Prize in Mathematics (2010)

- Polya Prize (2010)
- Crafoord Prize (2012)
- Simons Investigator (2012)
- Inaugural recipient of the Center for Excellence in Education's Joseph I Lieberman Award (2013)
- Breakthrough Prize in Mathematics (2015, awarded in 2014)
- Royal Medal (2014)
- Johns Hopkins CTY Distinguished Alumnus (2014)
- PROSE award (2015)

FURTHER READING

A Grenfell-Price, *Founders and Pioneers in South Australia*, Adelaide 1929.

AE Ridley, *A Backward Glance*, London 1904.

AJ Harrop, *The amazing Career of Edward Gibbon Wakefield*, Allen and Unwin, London, 1928.

Andrew Ramsay, *The Basis of Everything. Rutherford, Oliphant and the Making of the Atomic Bomb*, Kindle Books 2020.

C.Sturt: *An account of the sea coast and Interior of South Australia in C. Sturt; Narrative of an Expedition into Central Australia 1844-1845 London*, 1984.

Denise George, *Mary Lee*, Wakefield Press 2018.

Douglas Pike, *Paradise of Dissent, Longmans Green, London 1957*

DW Meinig, *On The Fringes of the Good Earth, The South Australia Wheat Frontier 1869-1884, Rigby, 1962*

E. Hodder: *The History of South Australia*, London 1893.

G Macfarlane, *Howard Florey*, Oxford 1979.

Geoffrey Dutton, *Founder of a city. The Life of Colonel William Light*, Rigby 1971.

J. Scott: *South Australia in 1887*, Adelaide 1887.

J.F. Bennett: *Historical and Descriptive Account of South Australia*, London and Edinburgh 1843.

J.L. Dow: *Agriculture in South Australia* by the Special Reporter of the Leader. Repeated for the leader. Melbourne & Adelaide, c. 1874.

J.P Stow: *South Australia: Its History, Productions and Natural Resources Adelaide, 2nd considerably expanded edition, 1884.*

Janis Sheldrick, Nature's Line. *George Goyder: Surveyor, Environmentalist and Visionary*, Wakefield Press 2014.

John Jenkin, *William and Lawrence Bragg: Father and Son*, Oxford University Press 2007.

Judith Brett, *From Secret Ballot to Democracy Sausage, The text Publishing Co, 2019*

Kristin Weidenbach, *Mailman of the Birdsville Track – the Story of Tom Kruse, Hodder, 2003*

Mary Estensen, *The life of Matthew Flinders*, Allan and Unwin 2002

Michael Langley, *Sturt of the Murray*, Robert Hale and Company 1969

Michael Molkentin, *ANZAC and Aviator: The Remarkable Story of Sir Ross Smith and the 1919 England to Australia Air Race*, Kindle Edition 2020.

R.Gouger: *South Australia in 1837 London 1839*, (Facsimile edition 1962)

Simon Nasht, The Last Frontier: *Hubert Wilkins, Australia's Unknown Hero*, Hachette Book Group 2011.

Stephen E Feinberg, *RA Fisher: An Appreciation*, Springer Verlag 1990.

Susan Magarey, *Unbridling the Tongues of Women, A Biography of Catherine Helen Spence*, University of Adelaide Press 2010.

The Critic: *The Land of the Golden Grain souvenir, Pinnaroo, Lameroo and Parilla. The new wheat growing Districts of South Australia. 1911*, Facsimile edition 1982.

W.R H. Jessop: *Flindersland and Sturtland* London 1862.

ABOUT THE AUTHORS

Allan Need was born in Adelaide and has lived in South Australia for most of this life. He graduated from Pulteney Grammar School in 1963 and gained a Bachelor of Medicine and Surgery degree from the University of Adelaide in 1970, after which he worked in London and New York. He is a trained Physician who was Head of Clinical Biochemistry at SA Pathology until his retirement in 2009.

A keen student of history, Allan gained a Doctorate from the University of Adelaide in 1981, is co-author of more than 129 research publications and has an interest in Medical Research Ethics. He enjoys South Australian red wine, water ski-ing and keeping up with his nine grandchildren who all live in South Australia.

Roger Henderson was born in Mount Gambier, south eastern South Australia. He trained and worked as a teacher in South Australia and the Northern Territory before becoming an A-class Principal and Education Consultant within regional and metropolitan R-12 schools in a career spanning 40 years.

He developed specialist language programs and teacher training within foreign language schools in Shenzen, China while working there for ten years. He authored four books, and numerous professional articles for curriculum leaders, parents and foreign teachers planning to teach English in Chinese State education facilities.

He is a proud South Australian with a strong interest in local history. Roger is a volunteer in several local community based organisations (Sustainable Living Communities, Renew SA, Blackwood Action Group, Blackwood Wine and Brewers, Wittunga Botanical Gardens and Voices of Boothby) and is an active supporter and advocate of everything South Australian.